To Deirdre and Richard,

BLOOD and BANDAGES

Fighting for life in the RAMC Field Ambulance 1940-1946

Best Wishes. William Earl
and
his Coward

BLOOD and BANDAGES

Fighting for life in the RAMC Field Ambulance 1940-1946

William Earl and Liz Coward

Dedication

For my comrades in the 214th Field Ambulance who never returned and all the men we couldn't save.

Copyright © 2016 Liz Coward

All rights reserved. No part of this publication may be reproduced, stored in a retrieval system, or transmitted, in any form, or by any means, electronic, mechanical, photocopying, recording or otherwise, without the prior permission of the publisher and copyright holder, nor be otherwise circulated in any form of binding or cover other than that in which it is published and without a similar condition including this condition being imposed on the subsequent purchaser.

Liz Coward has asserted the moral right to be identified as the author of this work.

Whilst every effort has been made to contact all copyright holders, the sources of some pictures that may be used are obscure. The authors will be glad to make good in future editions any error or omissions brought to their attention. The publication of any quotes or illustrations on which clearance has not been given is unintentional.

Designed and typeset by Philip Clucas MSIAD

British Library Cataloguing in Publication Data

A catalogue record for this book is available from the British Library

Published by Sabrestorm Publishing,
90 Lennard Road, Dunton Green, Sevenoaks, Kent TN13 2UX

Website: www.sabrestorm.com
Email: books@sabrestorm.com

Printed in Malaysia by Tien Wah Press

ISBN 9 781781 220085

Contents

Foreword 7
Introduction 7
1 The early years 10
2 Called-up 20
3 William and Frank 42
4 Enfidaville 54
5 The invasion of Italy ... 72
6 Frank's capture 89
7 Anzio 98
8 The price of friendship ... 108
9 D-Day Dodgers 120
10 Reunited with Mary 137
Epilogue 148
Glossary 150
Acknowledgements 151
Footnotes 152
Bibliography 156
Index 157

Blood and Bandages

Above: Recovering battle casualty while under fire.

Above: Preparing casualties for rapid evacuation to the main dressing station.

Foreword

*All I wanted to do was live the life that I wanted.
I was in love with Mary and wanted to start my life with her instantly, but first I had to get through the training, the landings, the Anzios and Frank's capture. That took six years.*
(William Earl, 16th January 2016)

Introduction

I thought I'd struck it lucky when I got my call-up papers. I'd been ordered to join a field ambulance in the Royal Army Medical Corps and, in those days, we all thought that a job with that lot was safe and easy. I thought I'd just be a male nurse and pick people up and carry them about on a stretcher. Had I known what a field ambulance actually did, I'd have been terribly upset. It was just like being in the infantry but without a rifle.

    The role of the field ambulance was to follow the infantry brigade to which it was attached. It collected, treated and evacuated the brigade's and all other wounded be they friend or foe. The field ambulance always had to remain mobile, so was organised 'to effect the rapid evacuation of the sick and wounded'[1] but was not equipped to provide anything other than 'the simplest accommodation and treatment.'[2]

It contained 238 men, 13 officers, 165 other ranks of the Royal Army Medical Corps (RAMC), 58 other ranks of the Royal Army Service Corps (RASC), a dental orderly, a chaplain and a chaplain's batman.[3] Most of the RAMC men were highly trained nursing orderlies who were taught to improvise and to work with a large degree of autonomy. Classed as non-combatants, they were protected by the Geneva Convention and as such, were entitled to wear Red Cross brassards on their forearms and display Red Crosses on their vehicles and treatment centres.

The most forward point of the field ambulance's responsibility was the regimental aid post, (RAP). Its position was chosen by the infantry unit's commanding officer, not the RAMC. The RAP lay just behind the front line. Although within range of enemy rifle and machine-gun fire, it had to provide rudimentary shelter for the wounded. Consequently, RAPs could be established in abandoned dugouts, disused trenches or behind large rocks and blankets could be tied to branches or trees to provide shelter from the weather. Around 40 injured men could be accommodated at each RAP[4] . The infantry's own regimental stretcher bearers (RSBs) were responsible for evacuating the wounded from the battlefield back to the RAPs. Incidentally, the regimental stretcher bearers were infantrymen and not RAMC personnel. As such, they wore 'S.B' brassards on their forearm unlike the field ambulance stretcher bearers, (nursing orderlies), each of whom was issued with a registered Red Cross brassard.

At the RAP the medical officer could administer basic first aid, check or apply a splint or tourniquet and give a morphine injection. A medical card would be fixed on the casualty's clothing before the nursing orderlies would, by any available means, evacuate the wounded back to the advanced dressing station, (ADS).

The route between the RAP and ADS was signposted. The ADS was 'established as far forward as military conditions will permit,'[5] often about 2,000 yards behind the front line and therefore still within range of medium artillery.[6] Unlike the RAP, the field ambulance chose the location of the advanced dressing station. It had to be accessible by ambulance and provide shelter from enemy shells and gas attacks. Therefore existing buildings were frequently commandeered or empty trenches adapted. If large numbers of battle casualties were anticipated, a walking wounded collecting post (WWCP) could be established behind the ADS for those able to walk despite their injuries.

The advanced dressing station could accommodate about 50 casualties. Only urgent treatment was provided such as surgery to control a haemorrhage.[7] Once treated and registered, the wounded soldier would be evacuated further down the line to the field ambulance's last unit, the main dressing station (MDS).

The MDS was the field ambulance's headquarters. It was located two to five miles behind the front line[8] and the wounded were ferried from the ADS to the MDS by two to four ambulances stationed near the former.[9] These were driven by the Royal Army Service Corps (RASC) and once loaded, departed with a nursing orderly riding shotgun in case the driver was wounded. If poor terrain or fighting restricted the ambulance's mobility alternative forms of transport would be used including sledges, mules and jeeps.

The main dressing station was located near a good road and water supply and was better equipped than the ADS. The MDS could accommodate 400 - 500 sick and wounded in buildings such as schools and hospitals.[10] At the MDS, patients were divided into two groups, those for evacuation and those to be retained. Evacuation cases were examined and urgent treatment given before being passed from the field ambulance's care to that of the RAMC casualty clearing station. Patients with minor injuries or ailments were retained to allow for a prompt return to their units. Nevertheless, it was undesirable for the MDS to hold onto casualties as that reduced its mobility. However, if the brigade was stationary, it could keep patients who were likely to recover within a week or so. Alternatively, it could open as a divisional rest station, (DRS) dealing with the sick especially those suffering from fatigue and strain.

Theoretically, a field ambulance's area of responsibility started at the RAP and did not stray beyond that point. However, in practice, the boundary was much more blurred.

In practice, we worked wherever we were needed and collected the wounded wherever they fell.

Blood and Bandages

Above: William Earl aged 3.

Above: William's parents, Bessie and Ernest Earl at Hastings August 1939.

Above: William, aged 16, May 1931.

Above: Mary Standen, aged 18, tennis courts Hastings August 1939.

1

The Early Years

William Ernest Earl was born on 12th May 1915 in a modest stone cottage on Long Melford Road, Sudbury, Suffolk.

Britain had declared war on Germany on 4th August 1914. By May 1915, the cost of war had been exposed and the appetite for glory had disappeared. Over one million French, Belgium and British soldiers had been killed, wounded or missing on the Western Front; [11] the Germans had launched the second battle of Ypres by bombarding French and British positions with 4,000 poison gas cylinders[12] and Sir Winston Churchill was on the verge of dismissal for the disasterous Allied landing on the Gallipoli Peninsular.

William was the family name and my Uncle William was fighting in the trenches on the Western Front. I was named after him in case he didn't come back. Uncle William survived the carnage and returned to England at the end of the war. He'd been gassed a couple of times so his lungs had been permanently damaged and he died young. My Dad wasn't allowed to fight for medical reasons so during the war he continued working as a silk weaver at the famous Gainsborough Silk Weaving Company.

Dad was a kind, considerate man who was ten years older than mum. My Mum was a lovely person but she was living in terrible poverty when he met her. She was the eldest of 14 children and spent all her time helping grandmother look after her younger siblings. It was an extremely harsh life. When Dad met and fell in love with Mum, she realised that he could be her means of escape from her life of drudgery, so when he proposed, she accepted. It wasn't hard because Mum liked Dad a great deal but she never managed to fall in love with him. After my birth she made it clear that she didn't want any more children. Instead, she showered all of her love on me. That was hard on Dad but he never took it out on me and we became close friends.

Our life in Sudbury was simple. We were poor but it didn't matter because that was normal. Dad wanted me to get a good education so he saved up to send me to a local private school. It was run by two ladies and the classes were really small. I liked it there, but had to leave when Dad was put on part-time work and couldn't afford the fees anymore. I joined the council school in North Street but didn't learn much there. When I was old enough I won a scholarship to Sudbury Grammar School. I was good at maths and loved figures so when I left in July 1931, I was offered an accountancy apprenticeship in a local firm. I was 16 and I was really looking forward to beginning my career. Unfortunately, my Father was made redundant before it even started so the following month we left to find work in London.

We moved in with my Aunt Alice's family at 23 Buckingham Road Harlesden. It was a small terraced house and we took over the downstairs by converting their dining room into a bedroom and using their lounge to store our furniture. It was snug but they made us feel very welcome.

Aunt Alice and Uncle Charlie had three children, two boys in their 20s and a 19-year-old girl called Agnes. Uncle Charlie was employed at Rotax, an engineering works in Park Royal. He put in a good word for Dad and got him a job as a general labourer. As I was 16, I also needed to contribute to the family income. I couldn't just wait around for another apprenticeship to come up so I answered an advert for a chemist's assistant at the local branch of Boots the Chemist.

I got the job and started on the 18th September 1931. For the first three months I was apprenticed to the manager as a general assistant. I followed him around the store and watched exactly what he did. Customers asked him about their illnesses and what medicines they should take. He advised them while I stood beside him taking it all in. Medicines were weighed or counted

Chapter 1 **The Early Years**

out, wrapped in the appropriate sized paper and carefully sealed with sealing wax so the ends of the paper wouldn't show. Occasionally, the manager asked me to serve someone and he'd listen to my advice to check that I said the right thing. For that, I got 12 shillings a week. I used to give 10 shillings to my Mother and spend the rest on sweets and a copy of the 'Boys Magazine.'
After a few months, I was told that I was good enough to become a chemist's assistant and was presented with a till, my own little gas jet, sealing wax and paper. The Londoners were so warm and friendly and I met lots of different people at Boots. Life was very easy going but I was still a simple country boy at heart so cousin Agnes decided to take me under her wing.

    She used to take me to the pictures and the variety shows at the Willesden Hippodrome. Sometimes she took me into Trafalgar Square and we'd see the sights. She was great. However, as time went on, it got a bit too cramped at their house especially when Aunt Alice invited their friends over. When that happened Mum, Dad and I used to keep out of the way and go and sit at the end of the garden. Nothing was ever said, but I think everyone was glad when, six months later, we moved into a rented house in Springfield Avenue. We stayed there for two years. Mum earned some money by taking in washing but after a while Dad gave up work at Rotax and started doing odd jobs. By that time, Mum's motives for marrying Dad had become clear and they started to argue. Eventually everything Dad did was wrong in Mum's eyes. I was still the apple of Mum's eye but I made sure that I was equally affectionate to both of them. In fact, I really enjoyed it when Dad and I went off to watch the football together. We both loved the game and although we were both Arsenal fans, occasionally we would watch other local clubs like Chelsea, Fulham, QPR and Brentford. Throughout this time I continued training at Boots. I studied various books on drugs and moved between branches to gain more experience. My wages had increased but eventually we couldn't afford the rent anymore. Luckily, Dad had a chance meeting with an old Sudbury friend who said that he was looking for a caretaker for their block of flats. The job came with free accommodation so Dad took it straight away.

    In 1934, we moved from Springfield Avenue Harlesden to the basement of

100 Addison Gardens Kensington. Mum became the designated caretaker and was responsible for keeping all the communal areas spic and span and the brass polished.

By 1937, William was 22-years-old. He had finished his training and was an experienced chemist's assistant working at the Bayswater branch. One day, a colleague, Rosie, asked William if he would like to join her group of classical music aficionados.

Rosie was stunning. She worked in the toiletry department selling perfumes and creams, (women weren't allowed to handle drugs). When she asked if I liked classical music, I said yes. I'd never heard any before but I wasn't going to tell her that and I was genuinely hooked the first time I heard Beethoven and Brahms. From then on my social life revolved around going to concerts with Rosie's gang and we always followed the same routine. On the morning of a concert at the Royal Albert Hall we'd troop off to the library, borrow the music scores and watch the concert from the gods while following the music. We became quite well known for it. That was the start of my love for classical music.

William's Mother, Bessie also had a love, the baptist church.

She got that from her mother. Grandma was so religious that we couldn't even have the radio on if we went to visit her on a Sunday. No, Sunday was a holy day and that was that. Mum wasn't that strict but she liked to go to two services on a Sunday. The nearest church was the Shepherd's Bush Baptist Tabernacle which was on the corner of Shepherd's Bush Green and Hammersmith Road. My parents went together on Sunday mornings and Mum and I went in the evenings. When we arrived, we'd split up. Mum went off to pray and I went upstairs to the balcony and listened to the choir while reading all the juicy bits in the Bible. Occasionally I'd glance downstairs and watch what was going on. That's when I first saw Mary. She was in the choir and stood out because she was young and very pretty. She wore a stylish Deanna Durban hat with a feather that bobbed around when she sang. I asked my mother who she was. "You want to keep away from her," Mum said, "She's got lots of boyfriends." Keeping away from her was the last thing

Chapter 1 **The Early Years**

Above: William and Mary at Hastings August 1939.

I wanted to do so I found out for myself. Her name was Mary Standen.

Bessie's objection wasn't just on the grounds of 'lots of boyfriends.' William's Mother had other plans for him and they included a demure, plainer member of the choir called Ivy Wilder.

Ivy was a lovely person but when I looked at her I thought, shall we go for a nice walk? When I looked at Mary, I thought, I'd just love to sleep with you.

That made no odds to Bessie.

15

The baptist church, with its' Mother's Union, tennis and youth club, was a social centre for its' parishioners. Therefore, Bessie grasped the chance to push William and Ivy together when it organised a fund-raising evening. However, William refused to go until his Mother casually mentioned that Mary would be performing there.

Then I changed my mind.

When we turned up, the church hall was packed. Mary, as usual, looked gorgeous and was beautifully turned out. She sang one or two songs while a chap called Cyril Cork accompanied her on the piano. I think Mary and Cyril were going out a bit at the time. When there was a lull in the entertainment, I spotted that Mary was on her own, so I plucked up the courage to go and speak to her. "I often see you at church." I said. "I often see you too," she replied, "You're very quiet." I didn't know what else to say so I said, "I like your hat." Then we parted company and rejoined our Mothers. For the next two years we only saw each other in passing and when I did, Mary was usually with Cyril.

That was exactly what Mary's Mother, Cissie Standen, intended. Cissi was an unsmiling and forbidding woman. Cyril Cork was her preferred choice for a son-in-law so William Earl certainly did not suit. However, luck was on William's side. In 1939, both Cissi and Bessie regularly attended the weekly Mothers' Union meeting. Although not friends, during a chance conversation, they discovered that they would be holidaying in Hastings at exactly the same time. When Bessie passed this on to William, he seized upon the opportunity to rekindle his acquaintance with Mary.

I played quite a lot of tennis and I knew that Mary belonged to the church tennis club so I asked my Mother to ask Cissie if Mary wanted to play when we were in Hastings. The answer came back in the affirmative. I was cock-a-hoop and a match was arranged for the Monday.

On Saturday August 26th 1939, Mum, Dad and I left London and arrived at our boarding house in Hastings. Everyone knew that each Saturday night there was a free concert in the bandstand on Hastings Promenade. It was the highlight of the week and everyone went. Mother said she was too tired to

Chapter 1 **The Early Years**

go but I insisted and off we trundled. Guess who was the first person we met? Mary, with her Mother and Grandfather. I was thrilled. There were some empty chairs beside them so we all sat together. It was hard to keep my mind on the music and not keep glancing at Mary. At the end of the evening, before we went our separate ways, I reminded Mary of our match the following Monday. Monday morning arrived and I turned up in my grey tennis flannels with my parents. By then, I was 24-years-old and Mary was 18. Mary arrived with her family. She wore a tennis dress and she looked smashing. After exchanging the normal pleasantries, we left our parents and walked up to the courts alone. I was just getting ready to play when Mary said, "Do you mind if we don't attempt this? I can't really play because it tires me out. I have heart trouble so I'm more of a social member." I thought that was odd so I asked her why she had agreed to play in the first place. She said she was interested in me because I was so quiet. I suggested that we had a cup of tea instead and we walked up to the café at the top of the hill, drank loads of tea and talked and talked.

Although she was five years younger than me and we'd never really spoken before, she put me at ease instantly. She was wonderful; so warm and friendly, charming and considerate. She was obviously a very loving and gentle person. Just talking to her made me feel happy and I felt as if I could tell her anything. She was sociable with a quiet and polite disposition and I thought she was the perfect young lady. It must have been at least two hours before we returned to our parents. We pretended that we'd been playing tennis the whole time and were worn out.

We managed to see each other again during the week but our parents were always there. One time, both families caught the little railway that took visitors to the top of West Hill. There we were, the Earls and Standens, sitting together on the rocks overlooking Hastings and enjoying the warm sunshine. My Dad had taken to Mary straightaway so he got out his little box camera and said to me, "C'mon, let's have a photograph of you both." I went and sat beside Mary but I was a bit shy so Dad said, "For goodness sake son, put your arm around her." So I did and he took a photograph. Cissie just sat there scowling probably thinking, that should be Cyril Cork sitting there, not him! She was such a dragon. I'm still amazed she could produce such a sweet, beautiful girl as Mary.

Mary and I hoped there'd be another opportunity to be alone together. Luckily there was a paddle steamer that stopped along the coast to pick people up and take them to Boulogne for the day. One of the stops was Hastings, so I asked Mary if she wanted to go. The Mothers were none too sure about the idea of us being unchaperoned but grudgingly gave us their permission to go.

We caught the steamer on 30th August and were so happy to be in each other's company again. When we disembarked we met some French people and they appeared very worried about the prospect of another war. They asked us what we thought. With the limited French she knew, Mary told them, yes, she thought there would be.

Understandably, for following his ascent to German Chancellor in 1933, Hitler had started dismantling the terms of the Treaty of Versailles imposed on Germany at the end of the Great War.

Subsequently, in 1935, Hitler ignored the term limiting the size of the German Army and reintroduced conscription. The term banning an air force was also reversed and the Luftwaffe came into being. Hitler sought and successfully obtained permission to extend the German Navy. In 1936, Germany reoccupied the Rhinelands and in 1938, annexed Austria and invaded Czechoslovakia. Desperate not to repeat the carnage of the First World War, Britain and France appeased Germany, even conceding control of the Sudentenland in Czechoslovakia, which effectively divided the country in two. The line was finally drawn in March 1939 when, despite assurances, Germany invaded the rest of Czechoslovakia. It was obvious that expansion into Poland was Hitler's next objective. Britain and France therefore announced that should Germany attack Poland, they would come to Poland's aid. Hitler responded with the Molotov-Rippentrop Pact with the Soviet Union. It was a state with which Hitler was idealogically opposed, but one which would allow him to fulfil his expansionist ambitions, if he, in turn, let the Soviets pursue their own. This non-aggression pact was signed on 23rd August 1939, with a secret protocol attached; namely an agreement to divide the Baltic States, Poland and Bessarabia into spheres of influence which would be unopposed by the other. Hitler agreed that the Soviets could have Estonia, Latvia, Lithuania and Finland, while Poland would be carved up between them. In return, the Soviet Union would supply Germany with essential goods like oil, grain and rubber. The pact was clearly a precursor to the invasion of Poland and Britain interpreted it as a cue to move onto a war footing.

But we were too happy to let the prospect of war dampen our spirits and we wandered off to a local café for ham and eggs.

On our return journey, we went below deck, found a banquette in the corner, cuddled up and fell asleep. We were still asleep when the ship moored up at Hastings. Our parents were waiting for us on the quayside and were getting more and more agitated when everyone disembarked except us. We woke up just before the steamer cast off and raced up the gangplank much to our parents anger and relief. That turned out to be the last steamer to France because the next day there was a sign at the end of the Pier saying, 'Due to the tension, all sailings will now stop.'

Twenty-four hours later, at 4.48am on 1st September 1939, Germany invaded Poland from the west.[13] Its' forces overwhelmed the country. Later that day, British and French representatives met with the German Foreign Minister to warn him that their countries would go to war with Germany unless she ceased hostilities and withdrew her troops. At 8.00pm, Poland requested immediate military assistance from Britain and France.[14]

We were due to return to London on 2nd September so both families had arranged to spend the last night together at a lovely big pub called the Carlisle. Mum, Dad and I arrived in good time and waited and waited, but the Standens never came. I was terribly upset and spent the rest of the night wondering why. There was still no message from them when we left for London on the Saturday.

The same day, Britain introduced conscription for all males aged between 18 and 41 and the Prime Minister ordered a general mobilisation.

An Evening With You.

Long are the hours the sun is above,
But when evening comes I go to my love.
She does not wait for me on the stair—
But runs to the door & greets me there.

As I enter the room, into my arms she comes,
& I kiss her face full of beauty & charm.
Then at her side in my usual place,
I gaze once again in her dear, dear face.

Aching & hot as my tired eyes be
She is all that I wish to see;
There as I sit, with her face touching mine,
I long for the day when she will be mine.

When the winter eves are dreary & cold
The firelight hours are a dream of gold;
& so I sit here with Mary, night after night,
In rest & enjoyment of loves delight.

And when the time comes for me to go
I tell dear Mary "I love you so".
Then I go home in the bright moon-beams
& of you my darling, have pleasant dreams.

Above: *An Evening with You* a love poem to Mary from William.

2
Called-up

Germany did not remove its' troops from Poland, so shortly before midnight on 3rd September 1939, an ultimatum was sent to the British Ambassador in Berlin ready for delivery to the German Foreign Minister at 9.00am.

At 11.15 am Neville Chamberlain, the Prime Minister, came on the wireless. He said, 'This morning the British Ambassador handed the German Government a final note stating that, unless we heard from them at 11 o'clock that they were prepared at once to withdraw their troops from Poland a state of war would exist between us. I have to tell you now that no such undertaking has been received, and that consequently this country is at war with Germany.'[15]

When the Prime Minister finished speaking the air raid sirens sounded across London but we didn't move. We just sat there looking at the wireless. Eventually we spoke. Dad took the news in his stride but Mother got very agitated. She thought that if the war lasted long enough, I would get called-up. Mum felt that if I were killed there would be nothing left for her to live for. She was so worried that she didn't even want to go to church. Instead, we spent the morning cutting up strips of brown paper and pasting them on to the windows. We were still at it at 12.15 pm when suddenly I saw Mary running down the steps to our basement. Mum was annoyed to see her on such a serious day as this. "It was just a holiday romance," she tutted. I ignored her, flung open the front door and embraced Mary on the doorstep. Mary was extremely anxious because my Mum never missed church so she thought I had been called-up. It was only the briefest of visits but Mary had time to explain that they'd left Hastings early because her Mother was worried about the threat of war.

Seeing Mary standing there, so full of worry, sealed it for us and we knew from then on that we wanted to be together. When she left, she gave me a present, a pair of socks. Mum saw them and thought Mary was mad. " It's not even your birthday!" she said.

The French government declared war against Germany within hours of Neville Chamberlain's broadcast. 'News of the double declaration of war…produced scenes of fierce joy in Warsaw.'[16] A succession of countries announced their own position on the forthcoming conflict. Unsurprisingly, those with close ties to Britain like Canada, India, Australia, New Zealand and South Africa were among the first to declare war on Germany. Others, such as the United States, Japan, Italy, Belgium, Holland, Luxemburg, Denmark and Norway declared that they would remain neutral.

The following day, 4th September, an advance party of the British Expeditionary Force, (BEF), landed in France. A further 158,000 troops arrived over the next five weeks.[17] The projected strength of the BEF by September 1940 was seven army corps.[18] To support them in battle, the Royal Army Medical Corps was required to provide 5,000 trained non-commissioned officers and men by the end of 1939, with a further 12,000 by September 1940.[19] Consequently, field ambulances were created, one of the first being the 169th field ambulance. The 169th was to form a very close relationship with the 214th field ambulance, the unit to which William was heading. Indeed, it was to the 169th that the men allocated to the 214th field ambulance were initially assigned.[20] As it was the BEF did not clash with the Germans until December 1939, an exchange which resulted in few casualties.

In fact, the French and British promises to come to Poland's aid came to nought. Neither country's forces were mobilised as the Poles expected. Instead, the British dropped propaganda leaflets over Germany and bombed the German naval base in Wilhelmshaven, while the French advanced onto German territory near Saarbrucken and halted. Many British citizens felt ashamed at this lack of aggression, unsurprisingly for 'the French and British had failed in their obligations shamefully.'[21]

Chapter 2 **Called up**

In the meantime, the courageous Polish army tried to fend for itself against a ruthless, well-equipped and contemptuous foe. Despite its outdated weapons and techniques, the Poles fought on bravely. However, the country's fate was sealed on 17th September when, in accordance with the secret protocol attached to the Molotov-Ribbentrop Pact, the Soviets attacked Poland from the east. The following year in western Poland, the Nazi regime began its policy of mass murder and perfected its' methods of annihilating lives 'unworthy of life'.[22] Eastern Poland experienced a similar level of brutality from the Soviets who used mass deportations and executions to crush all those identified with Polish nationalism and any who refused to be re-educated.

In contrast, from September 1939 to May 1940, Britain was virtually untouched by the seismic changes in central Europe. The anticipated enemy bombers failed to appear so evacuees returned home; cinemas and theatres gradually reopened and London pubs were packed. The most dangerous threat to life during this Phoney War was caused by the blackout which led to an increase in road accidents.

Mum still insisted on inviting Ivy around for tea but eventually she gave up and accepted that Mary was the one for me. From that point on she totally changed and did all she could to get Mary and I together.

Mary worked as a beautician at Adelaide Grey, a beauty salon on Bond Street. She lived with her Mother and Grandfather in a small terraced house just off Shepherd's Bush Green. I'd often go and visit Mary after work but her Mother, Cissie, was never that welcoming, probably because I wasn't Cyril, the preferred suitor. Mary's Granddad was very different. He was warm and friendly and I got on with him like a house on fire. He used to write little ditties which started with 'William and Mary.' Mary was very fond of him. Sadly, she never knew her Father because he'd emigrated to Australia before she was born.

Whenever I visited, we'd have some tea and then Mary would say, "I'm going up now to play the piano for William." We'd go to the upstairs lounge, leaving Cissie and Granddad in the kitchen.

Before my visits I'd write a little love poem to Mary based upon a popular verse of the day. I'd give it to her when we were alone. This is one of the ones that she kept until her dying day.

An Evening With You
Long are the hours the sun is above,
But when evening comes I go to my love.
She does not wait for me on the stair,
But runs to the door and greets me there.

As I enter the room, into my arms she comes,
And I kiss her face full of beauty and charm.
Then at her side in my usual place,
I gaze once again in her dear, dear face.

Aching and hot as my tired eyes be
She is all that I wish to see,
There as I sit, with her face touching mine,
I long for the day when she will be mine.

When the winter eves are dreary and cold
The firelight hours are a dream of gold
And so I sit here with Mary, night after night,
In rest and enjoyment of love's delight.

And when the time comes for me to go
I tell dear Mary, "I love you so."
Then I go home in the bright moonbeams
And of you, my darling, have pleasant dreams.

When we were alone like that, we'd have a kiss and cuddle but every 15 minutes or so Mary would say, "I'd better play the piano now otherwise my Mother will wonder what we're up to."

Chapter 2 **Called up**

Unfortunately, things were less happy in my home. Now that I was settled at Boots and had found my Mary, Mum felt her job was done and that it was time to create a life of her own without Dad. Gradually, it became clear by the way that she looked at Dad and spoke to him that she just wanted him to leave. I felt that he responded by starting to view me as a Mummy's boy.

By now, Mary had left Adelaide Grey and started working in a small dress factory near her home. William consequently changed his lunch hour to correspond with hers.

At 1.00pm I'd dash out of Boots and catch the bus to Shepherd's Bush to meet Mary on the Green. We'd have about 30 minutes to eat our sandwiches together before I rushed back to work. It was perfect, but at the back of my mind, I knew that at some point I would get my call-up papers.

Meantime, in April 1940, the Germans invaded neutral Denmark and Norway. Caught wrong-footed, the Danes quickly accepted the Nazi terms of 'peaceful occupation.'[23] The Norwegians resisted. However, even with Allied support, they failed to defeat the Nazis and remained under German occupation for the rest of the war.

On 10th May 1940, just as Winston Churchill replaced Neville Chamberlain as Prime Minister, the Germans launched a Blitzkreig, (Lightning War), and simultaneously invaded Holland, Belgium, Luxembourg and France. The speed, imagination and execution of the attack was devastating and the Allied forces collapsed under the onslaught. Within four days, there were eight million refugees on the road and Reynand, the French Prime Minister, rang Churchill to say, "We have been defeated."[24] The full extent of the Allied defeat became clear on the roads around Dunkirk and on 26th May, Operation Dynamo, the evacuation of the British Expeditionary Force from France, was launched.

The Admiralty only expected to remove 45,000 men from the beaches but the German advance had been so swift that it was halted outside Dunkirk to allow its' own infantry to catch up.[25] This gave the Allies more time to evacuate the besieged troops. Over the next nine days, 338,000 Allied soldiers were saved by the Royal Navy and an assortment of civilian vessels.[26]

The 167th field ambulance was among those who treated shiploads of French and BEF wounded who were being disembarked at the quaysides at Margate, Ramsgate, and Broadstairs. [27]

In late May 1940, just after Dunkirk, my call-up papers finally arrived.

Mum had been fearing the day and she sobbed and sobbed when she saw them. Dad was terribly bothered too but he kept calm. I was also concerned because Dunkirk was an eye-opener. After reading about all those soldiers left on the beach, the little boats and the number of men killed or injured, I realised, for the first time, how dangerous this war really was.

I was told to report to Euston Station on 2nd July, so Mary and I thought we could spend a week in Hastings before I left. My Mother didn't object because she wanted us to enjoy ourselves while we could, but Cissie was very unhappy about it, owing to the fact that we weren't married. After a lot of argument, she finally agreed but insisted that we book two single rooms. We did, but Mary spent the nights in my room then sneaked back to hers before the owner came up with the hot water for the washstands. During the day, we would walk along the Prom hand-in-hand or take the tram to the top of West Cliff. It was a wonderful week but the time soon came round for me to report to Euston Station.

Above: William and Mary in Hastings June 1940.

While William and Mary were enjoying their last week together, on 11th June 1940, Italy declared war on Britain and France. Two days later, the British

Chapter 2 **Called up**

11th Hussars crossed the Libyan border from Egypt and destroyed two Italian border forts and took 70 Italians prisoner. Of more immediate importance was the surrender of France on 18th June. The following day, Churchill told the House of Commons, 'What General Weygand has called the Battle of France is over; the Battle of Britain is about to begin. Upon this battle…depends our own British life, and the long continuity of our institutions and our Empire. The whole fury and might of the enemy must very soon be turned on us… Let us therefore brace ourselves to our duty and so bear ourselves that, if the British Empire and its' Commonwealth last for a thousand years, men will still say, this was their finest hour.'[28]

On the 19th June, the men allocated to the 214th field ambulance ceased to be attached to the 167th and moved to the 214th's own headquarters at Bunce Court near Otterden in Kent.

Mary was determined to see me go, so on 2nd July 1940, she took a day off work and came to my house to collect me. After a very tearful goodbye with my Mother, we left for Euston. I had to be there at 12 noon and when we arrived we saw loads of army trucks lined up outside. When we entered the station, there were about 100 chaps milling around and a small group of soldiers waiting for us. It got very emotional when the time came to say goodbye, but we knew that we would see each other again at some point.

After Mary left, I reported to one of the soldiers, a former 167th sergeant who formed part of the cadre for the 214th field ambulance. He said that I was assigned to the 56th (London) division, nicknamed the Black Cats because the divisional flash was a drawing of Dick Whittington's cat.

Once he'd filled in my details, I was told to get into one of the trucks outside. It was half empty when I climbed in and as I waited for it to fill up, I got chatting to the other men. Apart from the odd one or two, like the snake-cleaner from the circus, we were all either pharmacists or pharmacy assistants, so we wondered if they had slotted us into a role based on our civilian jobs. When the last man got on the tailgate was slammed shut and off we went. We didn't have a clue where we were going.

Under normal circumstances they would have been heading to Aldershot for basic training but because Germany was threatening to invade Britain from France, the 96 new recruits were put on immediate active service. Hence they were on their way to Bunce Court, the 214th's headquarters and arrived shortly before 5pm.[29] Their arrival marked the birth of the 214th field ambulance.

The 214th's purpose was to support their designated brigade of the 56th (London) division. The division had three infantry brigades, the 167th, 168th and 169th. The 214th field ambulance supported the 169th brigade. In July 1940, the 169th was made up of the 2nd/5th 2nd/6th and 2nd/7th of the Queen's Royal Regiment(West Surrey), 35th Infantry Brigade Anti-Tank Company, 3rd Coldstream Guards, 6th Grenadier Guards and the 169th(London)Infantry Brigade Anti-Tank Company. The men nicknamed it the Queen's and on 2nd July the Queen's were stationed in Kent, hence the location of the 214th's headquarters.

The day after their arrival, the commanding officer, Lieutenant Colonel (Lt-Col) Marshall, assessed the new recruits and noted in the war diary, 'Intake contains quite a number of men well trained in Red Cross work. Very good-looking set of men.'[30] On 4th July, the men were separated into X and Y training companies, kitted out and their civilian clothes were sent home.

Since the surrender of France, Hitler had offered to make terms with Britain. Churchill believed that this would reduce Britain to a slave state. He was therefore insistent that the country should refuse and fight on. Tired of this impasse, on 16th July, the Germans announced directive 16. Its' aim was to 'eliminate the English motherland as a base from which war against Germany can be continued, and, if this should become unavoidable, to occupy it to the full extent.'[31] The invasion was codenamed Operation Sealion and Hitler announced that an invasion force would be ready to set sail by 16th August 1940.

Under such circumstances, Lt-Col Marshall decided that parade drills

Chapter 2 **Called up**

should take second place to stretcher exercises, first aid and fieldwork.

I was put in X company. I trained during the day and at night camped in a little tent in the middle of a field watching out for German paratroopers. I had been armed with a pickaxe handle and a whistle. The whistle was to give a warning blast to the man in the next field who would blow his whistle to the man in the next field and so on until it reached the Queen's. What they expected me to do with the pickaxe handle, I never really knew.

Our lives had changed so completely. We were away from our loved ones and surrounded by strangers, living in tents and being yelled at. It was crazy but funny at the same time but going straight into the field like that meant friendship was really important. You needed someone you could talk to or even lean on in difficult times.

Our training was also intense. We attended lectures on anatomy, physiology and first aid and learned how to deal with broken limbs and shock. We practised camouflage and map reading and went on 20 mile route marches. We were taught about hygiene and sanitation and how to deal with gas attacks. We undertook stretcher exercises and watched demonstrations on casualty evacuation. We learned how to rapidly assemble and disassemble the main dressing station (MDS) and advanced dressing station (ADS) in daylight and darkness. We practised evacuating and loading casualties at night and were attached to local hospitals.

I was posted to Canterbury hospital where the nurses taught us how to assist them with their ward duties. We learned how to change dressings, take temperatures, administer enemas, diagnose minor injuries and judge the seriousness of wounds. We got gowned up to watch the surgeons operate in the operating theatres. I didn't flinch when they cut into the patients but some of the men went weak-kneed and a few fainted at the sight of so much blood.

At first, everyone was friendly to each other. Some I knew instantly weren't my sort of person. Others were always smoking and drinking and chasing the girls. They weren't my type either. I was just looking for someone with a like-mind but I never really found that until Frank Allen

29

joined in 1942. Until then I muddled along with men who were interested in things like football.

I occasionally got selected to play for the 214th's football team because I'd played for my local Stonebridge Park football team. Sport was important and being selected to play elevated your status to sportsman. By and large, sportsmen got more privileges than non-sportsmen so it was unlikely that sportsmen would get chosen for jobs like latrine or night duty. They also got to know the NCOs better like our Staff Sergeant Morgan. I turned out alongside him a few times and he gave me my army nickname, 'Duke'. Football was how I got to know most of my friends.

Staff Sergeant Morgan had come over from the 167th Field Ambulance and tried to teach us drill. We had problems with marching and about turn and he gave up in despair when he tried to teach us to slow march.

After six weeks, the NCOs had worked out which men worked best together and X and Y training companies were replaced by the standard field ambulance organisation of a headquarters with two companies, A and B.[32]

I was put in A company. A and B companies relieved each other, so when one was working at the ADS, the other was resting back at the MDS. This meant that we didn't see much of the other section so we tended to stick with our own.

The two companies were further divided into sections. Mine was A1 section and it included George Catchpole, Ronny Searle and Jack Farrington. George was very easy to get along with but was constantly chasing the ladies. Ronny Searle was Searle by name, surly by nature, but Jack Farrington was a nice chap and a very good footballer.

We went on exercise with the Queen's, and all the time it was drilled into us that we were not there to fight the enemy, our job was to save the wounded in accordance with the Geneva Convention. That meant that we had to treat all the wounded as if they were one of our own. Luckily, we weren't expected to drive the ambulances but we were taught how to in case our Royal Army Service Corps, (RASC), driver was killed. I wasn't very good at it and ended up in a ditch several times.

Chapter 2 **Called up**

Above: 167th Field Ambulance battle training course showing a casualty evacuated from a tree; taken across a river; evacuated using camouflage and removed from the second storey of a building. *(courtesy of the AMS Museum Aldershot)*

Before Germany could invade, the RAF had to be destroyed so its' army could sail across the Channel unmolested. The Luftwaffe therefore began testing the Royal Air Force's skill and response times by attacking convoys in the Channel. Once done, the main attack was launched. German bombers left their airfields at 5.10am on 13th August, Adler Tag (Eagle Day) intent on destroying the RAF. It marked the start of the Battle of Britain. From that day until 15th September 1940, fighter command, its radars and bases came under tremendous pressure from wave after wave of German aircraft. Fighter command 11 group covered the South-East and they took the brunt of the Luftwaffe attacks but were never defeated.

Everyday we witnessed the dogfights in the sky and it was terrifying to watch.

Frustrated by the lack of success, the Luftwaffe launched an all out assault on 15th September. That morning, 'a vast armada almost two miles wide' headed for England.[33] It was repulsed. There was another massive attack, 'in total, a combined force of 600 plus aircraft on a front of some 30 miles.'[34] Again they were checked. By the end of the day, it was clear that the RAF could not be defeated. With the failure to meet the first pre-requisite to invasion, Operation Sealion was postponed indefinitely. Instead, the Luftwaffe turned its focus on bombing London and industrial targets in the Midlands. The blitz had begun.

Meantime, William and his comrades were not only being trained, they were being smartened up and socialised. Appointments were organised for the dentist and barber; bath times were regulated; weekly dances were held in the village halls; cinema films were shown; sporting fixtures arranged and guest speakers invited to lecture on a variety of subjects.[35] In return, the men were expected to convert from a civilian attitude to a military. This was neither a quick nor easy transition.

We were all connected through health and medical work so we were all equal. Therefore we didn't salute officers when they walked by, we just said hello and got pulled up for it.

Lt-Col Marshall's patience was being tried and the men were constantly reminded not to wash their dishes in the bathroom; not to stamp their feet noisily during drills; not to take any souvenirs from crashed aircraft; not to remove any light bulbs, fittings, furniture, trees or shrubs without permission; not to stand in the middle of the road at night and hail a vehicle; not to ask other people to do their duties and not to visit the orderly room without permission.[36]

There were a lot of dos and don'ts and we hated it. We used to meet up in groups and say, "What did you think about that?" Or we'd go up to the sergeant and say, "What have we got to do that for? Why can't we do it this way?" Unlike the staff sergeants, the new sergeants were pharmacists so they were our former colleagues. Some, like Sergeant Abley, were great and you could talk to them man to man. Others would get on their high horse, pull rank and bark, "You can't say that, you're in the army now," or, "You can't do it that way because of army order number XYZ." They tried to treat us like we were in the infantry, but we weren't in the infantry and we weren't like the infantry. We viewed ourselves as civilian medical men first and soldiers second, so we felt quite justified when we complained about things that seemed nonsensical. And we complained about everything. Take meal times, five of us would sit around a table with a corporal or lance corporal and we would tell him exactly what we thought about the food. Just as the meal ended, the orderly officer would come around to each table and ask if everything was OK. The corporal would tell him what we'd said and it wouldn't make a jot of difference.

On 5th September 1940, the 214th moved the short distance from Bunce Court to Coles Dane House.[37]

Ten days later, Italy invaded Egypt, signalling the start of the North African Campaign. On 27th September, Italy entered into a Tripartite Pact with Japan and Germany. Five months later, Germany came to its' new Ally's aid when the Italian Army was routed by the British Army in North Africa.

Meantime, relations between Germany and the Soviet Union had deteriorated. The Nazi ideology was 'anti-Slav, anti-Communist and anti-semitic.'[38] Therefore, when relations between the two powers became strained, Hitler's prejudices re-emerged and he began to plan the annihilation of his Ally. William, oblivious that all three events would determine his future, was more interested in the affect of the blitz and rationing on Mary and his parents.

Sometimes, I'd get a 24 or 48 hour pass. Mary or my parents would catch the train from London and come to see me or I would go back home. One of my friends, Eric Holley, was a cheeky chap. He managed to get himself a job in the quartermaster's stores and whenever I went on leave he'd tell me to go and see him and he'd sneak two or three packs of butter and sugar into my kit bag.

The first thing I did when I got home was take off my uniform and put on my civvies. When I was dressed in my normal clothes I felt like the real me unlike some men who used to love strutting around in their uniform.

There was only so much we could do during my leave. On a 24 hour pass Mary and I would only have enough time to wander to Kensington Gardens, but on a 48 hour pass there was enough time to go to the cinema.

On 14th January 1941, after seven months of training, William sat his Nursing Orderly Class III exams.[39]

We were all examined at the end of our training, but only those with sufficiently high results and a demonstrable inclination to care for the sick, were designated the trade of Nursing Orderly Class III. I passed and could therefore undergo further training to become a Class II or Class I. Those that didn't pass joined other units like the Royal Engineers, the RASC or were given supporting roles within the field ambulance. The circus snake-cleaner, for instance, didn't pass, so his skills were used in the cookhouse to wash the pots.

I got my first long period of leave in February 1941. By then Dad had moved out. He felt that Mum would be happier without him and Dad loved her enough to leave. I missed him when he went.

There was more space when Dad left so Mary used to come over and stay with us. Mum was very fond of Mary and she knew that time was precious so she used to give us her bedroom and she'd sleep in the lounge on a put-u-up.

Chapter 2 **Called up**

Above: 214th Field Ambulance main dressing station, Coles Dane, Harrietsham September 1940.
Left: left top to bottom: Bob Haiselden, William Earl, F Agnew, Ron Luke.

    Upon the recommendation of his commanding officer, in May 1941, William began training for the higher qualification of Nursing Orderly Class 11.

    A month later, Hitler betrayed Stalin. Despite numerous intelligence reports warning of the attack, Stalin was shocked when Hitler launched Operation Barbarossa on 22nd June with the invasion of the Soviet Union by almost three million Germans troops. Working on the principle that my enemy's enemy is my friend, Churchill immediately began seeking an alliance with Stalin, even though he loathed the Bolshevik regime. Churchill's approaches were approved by the US and a Grand Alliance was formed between the United States, Britain and the Soviet Union to defeat their common enemy, Germany. It was an event which would push William overseas.

35

Mary and I had discussed getting married before I was called-up but we had decided to wait until the war was over. When I found out that I was going abroad, I said to Mary, "I may not come back but I would love to be married to you even if it was for a little bit and as a soldier's wife you'd also get a small amount of money each week." It wasn't very romantic and I didn't have a ring but she said yes anyway. When I got back to barracks, I asked to see the commanding officer and told him that I wanted to get married before we left. He thought that was a very good idea and said that he'd give me as much leave as he possibly could. Later, I was informed that I could have five days starting on 28th November. I told Mary and we set a date for Saturday 29th November 1941 at our regular church, Shepherd's Bush Baptist Tabernacle. I left it to Mary and my Mother to make all the arrangements.

They saved up all their ration cards and ordered a cake from T. P Lock and Co. The invitations came from Cissie, and Mary was so excited that she sent some of them out in the wrong envelopes! I was just as thrilled. I even got a letter from cousin Roy, saying that, 'he too would be excited if he were about to be married to the young lady, that invincible she, the inspiration of one's life and the chief subject of one's thoughts and wishes.'

However, in the middle of the preparations, William received a letter from Mary.

She told me that she was three months pregnant. Cissie was very angry and blamed my mother because Mary stayed with us when I was on leave. Cissi insisted that Mary could not wear a white wedding dress, as she wasn't a virgin. If Mary did, Cissie would not come to the wedding. Mary was terribly upset.

Whilst emotions ran high at the Standen's, orders were received for the Black Cats to leave Kent and move to the Ipswich area. Consequently on 16th -17th November, the 214th began its two day journey across Kent, London and Suffolk to St John's Children's Home in Ipswich.[40] On 28th November, William left the main dressing station to spend his last night as a bachelor at his Mother's house in Kensington.

Chapter 2 **Called up**

Shortly after I arrived, I went to see Mary and gave her a letter with the strict instruction that it could not be opened until the next morning.

Dear Mary,

When you get this my darling, I shall be at the church waiting for you to claim you as my own forever to the whole world. I am gloriously happy, no-one could be more happy than me, as very soon darling, you, the Most Glorious and Most Wonderful girl alive will become my darling wife. I do love you madly and always will...

So darling I wait for you with all my love and all I possess.
Always and ever yours Will

Inside was a little poem.

To you my dearest darling
All my dreams and hopes of you
On this the great day of my life,
Will be fulfilled and will come true
When you become "my darling wife."

I vow to you with all my heart
And mind and soul that come what may
My love for you will never end,
But will grow stronger every day.

And so my dear, on this "Our Day"
My heart and soul it is all thine,
All I have at your feet I lay
I am all yours, and you are mine.

And as we live our lives together,
So my first thoughts will always be,
Of you, your joy and happiness,
I will always love you, dearest Mary.

Blood and Bandages

Above: William and Mary's wedding party 29th November 1941
Back row left to right: Ted Boggis, Joy Ransom, Mary's best friend, Eric Sanders.
Front row left to right: Bessie Earl, William Earl, Mary Earl, Cissi Standen.

The wedding was at 1.00pm and the church was full. Eric Holley and Bob Haiselden, another army friend, got some leave to come. Cyril Cork and Ivy Wilder's parents were also there but sadly Dad wasn't.

Mary had bowed to Cissie's threat not to come if she wore white, and was wearing a maroon dress. Only the Mothers knew about the pregnancy and they weren't going to broadcast it, so we decided to blame the rationing if anyone passed comment about the colour of the dress. Even then Cissie wasn't happy. She'd set her heart on Mary marrying Cyril Cork but he was sitting in the congregation, not standing at the altar.

Chapter 2 **Called up**

Afterwards, 50 of us sat down to a meal at Slaters and Bodega, a smart restaurant on High Street Kensington and enjoyed thick mock turtle soup, roast chicken and trifle washed down with haut sauterne and port.

After the reception, Mary and I caught a train from Liverpool Street to Chelmsford so we could honeymoon at my Uncle Harry and Aunt Eva's. They were caretakers of a big Presbyterian church and very upright people. When the time came for Mary and I to go to bed, Aunt Eva took Mary to one side and said, "I think you'd better have something strong to drink before you go upstairs. It's going to be quite emotional for you." After Mary had had a drink, Aunt Eva solemnly told Mary to go upstairs and let her know when she was ready to receive me. Mary did as instructed and I was sent upstairs. Mary was in fits of laughter by the time I entered the room.

My leave ended at midnight on 2nd December and I reported back to the guardroom just in time. They said, "Did you have a good honeymoon? You must tell us all about it. Well don't tell us all about it and by the way, you're playing football tomorrow." "How do you expect me to play football after a five day honeymoon?" I said, but that made no difference. If you were picked, you played. So the next day, I pulled on the yellow jumper that Mary had knitted for me and played my worst ever game of football.

On 8th December 1941, the war took a major turn. An outraged and grieving United States declared war on Japan in response to the previous day's devastating attack on the United States naval base at Pearl Harbour and the American oilfields in the Philippines. On 11th December, Germany and Italy declared war on the United States in accordance with the terms of the Tripartite Pact. In response, the United States declared war on Germany and Italy. Although this event was to have a direct impact on William, he was focused on his impending departure.

Mary's 21st Birthday was on 31st March and I was so thankful that I managed to spend it with her in Ipswich. Although she was seven months pregnant by then, I didn't really take much notice. Then on 21st May, I was on parade when the sergeant major came across the road and said, "Duke, fall out and come here." I followed him across the parade ground and he said, "I've just had a message from the orderly room. You've become the father of a boy. Congratulations." I was stunned. "Oh. Thank you sir," I said and turned on my heel and returned to the parade ground. It hadn't really sunk in that Mary was pregnant, so it felt as if I had just walked into a room and someone had picked up a baby and announced, "This is your son." I felt no connection with him at all and that worried me because that didn't feel right. A few of us went down to the local pub that night to celebrate, but I found it very difficult to acknowledge to myself that I had a son. I managed to get two 48 hour passes before we left so I leapt on a train to London and went to see them. David and Mary lived with Cissie and Granddad but they came and stayed at my Mother's when I was on leave. I had a chance to cuddle David before he was whisked away so that Mary and I could have the remaining hours alone together. I didn't object, because I still didn't see myself as a father. Little did I know that the next time I'd see David he'd be four-years-old.

By now, William had achieved the higher qualification of Nursing Orderly Class 11 and the 214th was making its' final preparations for action overseas.[41] Men considered unsuitable for action, like the snake-cleaner, were weeded out and others, like Frank Allen, were transferred in.

Frank was a few years older than me but we clicked instantly over our love of football. He was a semi-professional footballer for Kettering Town and had turned out alongside the great Arsenal back, Eddie Hapgood. For an Arsenal fan like me, that was gold dust. Frank was a big bear of a man but he was mild and always spoke slowly and carefully. He never panicked, nothing ever annoyed him and he never, ever, had a bad word to say about anybody. The sergeants saw how well we'd hit it off so they put him in A1 section and we were paired up as a team.

In August 1942, Churchill gave orders for the destruction of the German-Italian (Axis) Army in Egypt and Libya. The 214th was put on stand-by and all leave was cancelled.[42]

I used to play a little bit of chess before the war so when I knew that we could go at any time I made myself a cardboard chess set with slots for the

Chapter 2 **Called up**

Left: William, Mary and David June 1942.

pieces. It was small enough to fold up and put in my top pocket and it went with me everywhere. Then on the night of 28th August 1942, they said, "Right, pack up. We're moving out." Within hours we were loaded up and on our way to Lavenham Station. Two trains were awaiting our arrival and we departed for Liverpool to join the rest of the division.

Frank and I sat together making out the shapes of the towns and villages we passed. I felt relieved. The war had interrupted my life and I wanted to get it over and done with as soon as I could so that I could return to Mary and David. It had been going on for almost three years and we felt it couldn't go on for much longer. We'd be the ones to help finish it.

After we'd detrained at Liverpool Exchange Station, we marched to the docks. Waiting on the quayside was RMS Franconia, one of Cunard's transatlantic liners that had been requisitioned and converted to a troopship. We embarked and said good-bye to England.

Blood and Bandages

Above: Frank Allen, left back row and William Earl, right back row with comrades in the Tunisian desert.

3
William and Frank

RMS Franconia II left Liverpool on 28th August and headed north to join a convoy which was gathering off the coast of Glasgow. When all the vessels had assembled, the convoy left the relative safety of British coastal waters and sailed into the Battle of the Atlantic, 'the largest, longest and most complex battle of World War Two.'[43] As an island nation, almost everything that Britain needed came across the Atlantic from her Colonies, the Commonwealth and America. Therefore, Germany thought that by sinking the merchant ships that kept Britain 'fed, fuelled and fighting,' it would starve Britain out of the war.[44]

It was a battle that pitted the wits of Allied merchant and naval fleets against German u-boat submarines and since the surrender of France in May 1940, the Nazis had had the advantage of access to France's submarine bases. Their most feared tactic was the use of wolfpacks, groups of German u-boats which assembled together to launch an attack on a selected target.

The impact of these was lessened by a combination of permanent naval escorts for merchant vessels and the use of convoys, but the real breakthrough came in February 1941. The Germans used Enigma, a complex secret code to communicate with each other and in February 1941, a German naval enigma machine with a complete set of ciphers was captured. This eventually enabled the enigma code to be cracked and the messages telling the u-boats where to assemble could be deciphered. As a result, Allied shipping was steered away from them and the tonnage lost duly decreased. Unfortunately, as a result the German Navy became suspicious that its' codes had been cracked. Therefore, in February 1942, enigma's security was improved by introducing a fourth rotor to the enigma machine. The naval codes became indecipherable once again and the wolfpack kill rate increased. This new naval enigma code had still not been cracked by the time William's convoy set sail from Scotland.

As a precaution, they split the division into two convoys. The men were in one and our arms and equipment were in the other so if the worse happened they wouldn't have lost everything.

Over five thousand of us were crammed into the Franconia. The 214th was allocated its' own area and there we ate, slept, tended to the sick and continued our training. There was hardly any room so we had to take our chances where we slept. I found a place under a mess table and Frank secured the one next to me. We were already good friends but we only got to know each other properly onboard.

We discussed lots of things, like our early years, sport, music, our jobs, and how we met our wives. We swapped photographs of our loved ones and I was surprised to see that his wife, Marjorie, looked like a female version of him. As we got to know each other, it became clear that we had the same modest attitude to life. Unfortunately, it was one that most of the other men didn't share. They just thought Frank was boring; he didn't smoke or drink excessively, wasn't on the take and was only interested in his wife. Sometimes, Frank and I would try to find a quiet space where we could talk more easily and get away from the crowds. On deck was the best place. We'd sit there and talk as we watched the waves or the sun setting over the sea. We knew there were wolfpacks under the sea waiting to blow us to kingdom come but what could we do about it? We'd have scant chance of survival if they did so we just sat back and enjoyed each other's company.

Frank lived in Northampton with Marjorie and worked as a boot and shoemaker in the local boot factory. He didn't have any children and it seemed to me that his whole life revolved around football, his wife and his job. Apart from his football, I don't think Frank had much experience of life. However, he was keen to learn about life outside so I'd tell him about the classical concerts I'd gone to with Rosie, about sightseeing with cousin

Chapter 3 **William and Frank**

Agnes, and parades like the Lord Mayor's Show. He'd listen intently, nod his head and smile. I still carried my chess set in my top pocket and when we grew tired of talking, I'd teach him a few simple moves. We ended up playing a lot of chess. We developed a deep and lasting bond during that journey and I felt he was someone that I would have happily embraced as a real brother.

When we docked at Freetown, we found out that a wolfpack had attacked the other convoy and had sunk the ship carrying all our equipment. We thanked our lucky stars that it hadn't been us, but a division without arms or equipment was useless so we were out of action until we could be re-equipped.

The division continued onto Cape Town, South Africa. King George V was its' head of state and, after the deposition of the anti-British Prime Minister, the country had declared war on Germany in September 1939. Its' new Prime Minister, Jan Smuts, had become an important adviser to Winston Churchill and thousands of white, coloured and black citizens had joined the Allies. The Franconia therefore sailed into a friendly harbour and after almost a month at sea, the men were given shore leave which was, 'much enjoyed by all ranks.'[45]

Each morning, Cape Town's white inhabitants would line the quayside to meet us as we came off and anyone who was on their own would be invited to be their guest for the day.

Frank's employers in Northampton had opened up a boot factory in Cape Town and Frank knew the man who'd moved there to manage it. Frank made enquiries and found him almost straightaway. From then on, this man collected us and took us back to his home where we'd be served with gorgeous food by his black servants. That disturbed Frank and I a bit because we felt that the servants were being treated like the underdog when Africa was their country, not the white man's. We did a bit of sightseeing but at midnight we had to return to sleep onbord the Franconia. One morning, hundreds of us decided to get up early to see the sunrise over Table Mountain. It was a super sight.

Meantime, for safety and security reasons the 214th was divided in two.

Half were sent on their onward journey by land, whilst the rest remained in Cape Town.[46]

We'd been in Cape Town for about a week, when one night we returned as normal only to be told that we were sailing the next day. "Where are we going?" we asked. "You'll know when we set sail." That was that. No one was allowed off after that because they didn't want us to tell anyone in case there were spies around. We never had the chance to say thank you and goodbye to Frank's friend.

However, it was a wise precaution. Not all South Africans were in favour of entering the war and some, particularly amongst the Afrikaner community, supported the Axis forces.

When we were at sea we were told that we were off to Bombay. We thought, Oh no. We're headed for the Burma Front to face the Japs.

Since 1937, Japan had aggressively pursued its policy of unification against western imperialism and China. As such, British held Burma was seized by Japanese and Thai forces in May 1942. The Allies wanted it back but lacked sufficient resources to campaign on two fronts. The Middle East Front was given priority and unknown to William, it was to this theatre that the 214th was heading. It arrived in Bombay harbour on a warm October day but their reception contrasted starkly with that which they had received in South Africa.

There was no one to meet us at the quayside. We just disembarked and marched through the city to our transit camp on the outskirts. We only stayed there for two days and on the second day we were allowed to go into Bombay for a few hours.

It was dirty and it stank but it was the poverty that took my breath away. I'd known poverty at home but nothing like this. I just couldn't take it in. This wasn't living, not as I knew it, and the children, helpless and hopeless children, lay in the gutter covered in dirty rags. Some had an arm or leg missing. You tried to give them some of your rations, but they needed more to eat than chocolate. The markets were worse. They were selling young girls in cages just like we sold chickens at home. I'd never seen, then or since, such degrading scenes as I saw in Bombay. I couldn't wait to get back to camp.

Chapter 3 William and Frank

Shortly after that, the division split up. Our unit, along with some infantry companies, boarded some old steam trains and were taken up to transit camp Deolali.

On 23rd October, they were joined by half the 167th field ambulance, which had also been split up at Cape Town. Ex-167th men, like Eric Holley and Sergeant Major Morgan were reunited with their old comrades and the inter-ambulance football rivalry hotted up.[47]

Deolali was a peacetime service camp and whoever wrote, 'It Ain't Half Hot Mum' must have been there because the camp looked exactly the same. There were wooden huts and Indian servants waiting in the shade ready to tend to our every need. There was one to shave us, another to clean our equipment and at 3pm the char-wallahs would suddenly appear. They had great big tea urns on their backs and they'd go around yelling, "char-wallah, char-wallah" and we'd all rush out of our huts clasping our tin mugs to get a lovely cup of tea.

We kept training of course; route marches into the hills to get fit again; lectures on medicine and medical care; stretcher bearing exercises; practising how to treat broken legs, stop haemorrhages, and the use of splints. We couldn't do much else without our equipment so when the training was done we were entertained with open air films. Occasionally, one or two men in our company would dress up as women and put on a little musical performance.

Their stay at Deolali was short-lived for on 1st November, the men were ordered to pack up and return to Bombay for their onward journey.

Meanwhile, on 8th November, British and American troops landed in Tunisia and Morocco as part of Operation Torch, the first joint Anglo-American endeavour of the war.

When we arrived at Bombay harbour, we boarded HMT Lancashire. Again, we thought we were off to Burma but then we found out that we were heading for Iraq.

In May 1941, Britain had invaded Iraq following a coup d'etat which had replaced a pro-British government with one which supported nationalism and

Blood and Bandages

Above: 56th (London) Division's divisional flash, Dick Whittington's black cat.

the Axis (joint German-Italian) forces. The victorious British restored a pro-British government and continued to use the unlimited rights, (which Britain had ceded to itself), to station and transit troops through the country without consulting the Iraqi government. Hence, HMT Lancashire arrival at Margil Port, Basra, on 11th November en route to Tunisia.[48]

When they disembarked the 167th and 214th parted company. The 167th proceeded to the Shuaiba second independent PoW camp,[49] while the 214th stayed at PoW camp Azubair before entraining to Baghdad to catch an onward train onto Kirkuk.[50]

The train was very old and rusty and frequently stopped to take on water. When it did, we'd all leap off the train and run up to the engine driver to ask him if we could take some hot water to make tea. He usually said yes. Once we drew off so much water that the train stopped working. We had to wait for another engine before we could proceed with our journey. I thought it was quite funny that the British Army had been brought to a standstill by cups of tea.

They arrived in Kirkuk on 19th November and were slowly rejoined by hundreds of Black Cats who had travelled by land from Cape Town.

As the whole division of the Black Cats reassembled in the desert, each regiment built its own accommodation, the 214th creating a tented village with trench latrines, sewage pits, stores and a mess area.

By 22nd December, all the 214th's officers and men had returned, so training could re-start in earnest. Exercises with the Queen's were undertaken; courses were held on malaria control and tropical diseases; and there was a cross-country route march of 38 miles in 33 hours with light medical equipment. The unit gave a demonstration of the layout and working of the main dressing station (MDS) to the division and there was a mutual exchange of officers with other medical units, such as the 37th Indian field ambulance.[51]

Not surprisingly, all this activity did not go unnoticed.

The locals cycled up to the camp and tried to sell us things like eggs and walnuts. They also offered to show us places that had been mentioned in the Bible. We had plenty of rest time so a group of us went off with them to see the sights.

We visited a very, very old church and inside there was a tomb which was supposed to be the tomb of Daniel, the one who was thrown in the lions' den. The tomb was surrounded by railings and attached to them were hundreds and hundreds of rusty old padlocks. The local guide told us that when a woman became pregnant she would visit the tomb to pray that her baby would be a boy because girls meant nothing to them. After praying, the woman would put a padlock on the railings as if to say, I've been here and you've promised that I'm having a boy so I'm going to keep you to your promise with this padlock.

Another time, we went far out into the desert to see the Fiery Furnace, again the one that was mentioned in the Book of Daniel. They dared us to go and stand in the centre, so we did and after about five minutes our feet suddenly got really hot. We were jumping around and trying to scrape away the top layer of sand but underneath it was even hotter.

The division remained in Kirkuk for four months and continued training whilst their supplies and equipment were replenished. Meantime, on 14th January 1943, Allied leaders met in Casablanca to discuss, amongst other matters, the cross-Channel invasion of France and further engagements in the Mediterranean. Neither side saw eye-to-eye. The Americans wanted to invade France as soon as possible following the military principle that, 'an attacker should go the shortest route to his objective with the greatest strength he can muster.'[52] Churchill agreed, but only when success was assured. He believed that, until then, the Allies should extend their operations in the Mediterranean to weaken the Germans and force them to withdraw divisions from the Eastern Front; to protect the sea route to India; to encourage resistance in the German occupied Balkans; to cut off essential supplies to the German Army and to billet non-communist troops in central Europe.

After ten days of heated exchanges, the cracks were papered over. It was agreed that the return to France would be delayed until 1944, by which time there would be sufficient ships and landing craft and the Allied troops would be trained and battle-hardened. Meantime, they would invade Sicily after the Axis troops had been defeated in Tunisia.

Chapter 3 **William and Frank**

Back in Kirkuk, 21st March saw the Black Cats fully equipped and ready to move off to join the Eighth Army in Tunisia. By this time, the North African campaign was in its' final phase. Following the Allied victory at the second battle El Alamein on 2nd November 1942, the Axis forces had disobeyed Hitler's orders and retreated west. The Eight Army had given chase across Egypt and Libya, and following the British and American landing in Algeria and Tunisia on 8th November 1942, the Allies were now in front and behind the Axis forces. It was only a matter of time before the demoralised and under-resourced troops were defeated. Not surprisingly, morale was high amongst the Allies as the Black Cats raced to join them for the final push.

They said it was the first time a whole division had ever moved in one convoy at the same time and it stretched back for hundreds of miles.

Indeed, it was so long that the 214th had crossed the boundary between Paiforce, (Persia and Iraq Forces), and the Mediterranean Expeditionary Force, (MEF), some 150 miles away, before the 167th field ambulance had even left Baghdad.[53]

It was an awful journey. We spent days in the back of our trucks being jolted across rough desert tracks. If it rained black oil rose up through the sand to the surface and the roads became as slippery as ice. There were so many flies, but I hated the sandstorms most of all. You could see them rolling in towards you and no matter what you did, the sand got everywhere. You could have a ration biscuit in your hand but by the time it got to your mouth it was covered in sand and that caused a lot of diarrhoea.

Each night we stopped to camp. We'd put up our bivouacs while the cooks set up the kitchen and the man in charge of latrine duty would go to the edge of the camp and start digging a trench. Sometimes the sergeant major would pick some men to help him but they probably wouldn't be sportsmen, more likely to be conscientious objectors. Frank and I knew there were a couple in the unit. We didn't know who they were but it was known that conscientious objectors tended to get the dirty jobs or tidy up the odds and ends back at HQ.

Blood and Bandages

For five days, the unit travelled an average of 130 miles a day and by 31st March they had reached Tulkran in Palestine where they briefly rested.

Jerusalem was not too far away so Frank and I hitched a lift and visited the city and some other holy places. It was also Mary's birthday so I hoped that she'd got the letter I'd written en route.

My own dearest beloved Mary,

Last year my darling, I was able to be with you on your birthday, but this year I am hundreds of miles away from you… and longing to be with you on your 22nd birthday… I am always thinking of you my beloved, every minute that passes, but on the 31st you will be in my heart and thoughts more than ever, darling. How wonderful it would be if I could spend the day by your side, yet it has to be otherwise; I could not get a card for you out here, so I am sending one of my own on another air graph…with the earnest prayer that next year we shall be together in our own home…

Yours alone, always and forever, your ever loving husband.

The next day, they rejoined the convoy and on 22nd April the 214th finally arrived at Hergla, twenty miles from the front line.[54]

By the time the Black Cats joined the Eighth Army, 'the Boches were nicely boxed up in the north-eastern corner with a line running from Bizerta round through Medjez-el-Beb to the coast to Enfidaville.'[55] Enfidaville itself had been captured on 19th April but strong resistance had been encountered on the outskirts. Within 24 hours of their arrival, the Queen's were ordered to advance towards the front line to help eliminate the opposition.

Consequently, three of A company's sections, including William and Frank's, were instructed to follow and set up a casualty collecting post (CCP), four miles south of Enfidaville.[56]

We followed the Queen's wherever they went.

Hence, on the 23rd April 1942, William finally went into action.

Chapter 3 **William and Frank**

Above: Damaged photograph of Mary Earl (nee Standen) which accompanied William overseas.

Above: A main dressing station in a ravine in the Western Desert during the North African Campaign.

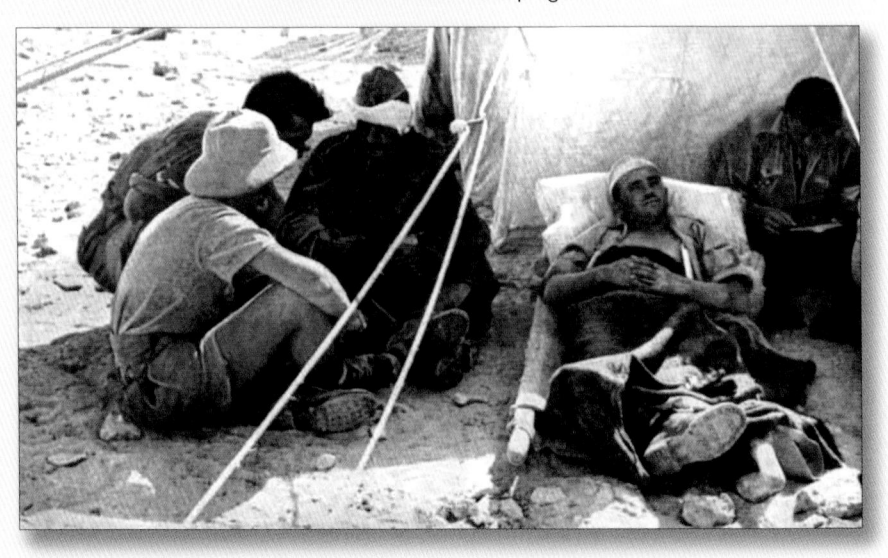

Above: Allied and Axis wounded rest after treatment at an advanced dressing station in the desert.

4
Enfidaville

We clambered onto the lorries and travelled alongside our ambulances at the rear of the convoy. We hung back because if we got too close to the infantry, we could get caught up in enemy fire.

Enfidaville's distant woodlands stood out on the hot dry savanna plain. Limestone mountains and hills lay to the north, salt mashes to the south-west and the gulf of Hammamet to the east. Nearby, Takrouna village had, after bitter fighting, just been won by the Allies and the dead were still being recovered when the 214th advanced.

As we trundled along the dirt track, we wondered what was going to happen and how we would react when we went into action. Would we cower away? Would we be afraid? Would we be cowards? Would we risk our lives? None of us knew what we would do. The speculation faded as the sound of the guns got louder and we came within range of the enemy's artillery.

Reinforcements were an obvious enemy target, so as we got closer to the action the Queen's started to spread out and we slowed down. The Axis forces opened fire the moment they spotted our troops and the advance stopped. When we looked out from under the flaps we were horrified to see that three or four of our ambulances had gone ahead and had got mixed up with the infantry. We looked on helplessly as we saw our ambulances get caught in the middle of the shelling zone. We later learned that when the firing had started, one of our comrades had been so scared that he had frozen to the spot. A shell detonated beside his ambulance and shrapnel tore through its' skin straight into his body. He was killed outright. It was very sobering to know that before we'd even gone into action, one of ours had been killed.

For two years, we'd been meticulously drilled on how to respond when we were under fire. We'd practiced with the Queen's firing blanks at us while our sergeant majors screamed, 'GET DOWN! LAY DOWN!' However, after that first encounter with the Axis troops, we suddenly realised that being well trained and well disciplined was one thing, but being able to react correctly when our brains were screaming at us to freeze or fly, was quite another. In fact, some of the men caught up in the bombardment suffered a bit of shell shock. That first foray towards the front line affected quite a lot of us because we saw what being in action really meant. It meant that we were on our own and if we made the slightest mistake we could be killed instantly. No amount of training could prepare us for that.

In light of the attack, A company was ordered to set up the casualty collecting post, (in essence a forward advanced dressing station), two miles further back.[57]

When we went forward again, the mood in the lorry had changed. All we thought about was keeping together, helping one another and looking after each other so that we had a greater chance of survival. We drew to a halt at our new location and disembarked. Our sergeant split us up into groups of four. Some set up in nearby ditches and wadis. As always, Frank and I were together and we dug a trench amongst the trees with our short handled spades, one of our most essential pieces of kit.

Our casualty collecting post, (CCP), was the closest medical unit to the fighting. Further in front of us were the 169th brigade's own regimental aid posts, (RAPs), which was run by a regimental doctor.

When the fighting started, the regimental stretcher bearers, (RSBs) picked up the injured and tried to get them back to the RAPs. They left them there and went back for more while the regimental doctor examined them. He gave them basic first aid and kept them warm. If he had time he'd administer morphine or apply a tourniquet. We then went forward to evacuate the wounded back to our casualty collecting post so that the RAPs didn't get clogged up. If the CCP was closer than the regimental aid post, the regimental

Chapter 4 **Enfidaville**

Above: British troops search for Axis forces in Enfidaville before engaging in bitter fighting in Takrouna.

stretcher bearers would bring the casualties straight to us and we'd treat them with basic first aid with the supplies we carried in our satchels. When there was a rapid advance, the RSBs would leave the wounded behind for us to collect as they were infantrymen who had to follow their own unit.

We never knew what type of injuries we would encounter. Sometimes, we would find a soldier screaming in agony because half his leg had been blown off. Other times, we'd attempt to carry a man but when we grabbed his arms, one of them would come off in our hands. Some men were so badly injured all we could do was make them comfortable and leave them to die. It was grim, but this was what I'd been trained to do and I felt that if I couldn't do that, then I shouldn't be doing this work. Of course, a big part of our job was to hide our feelings. It would have been unforgivably cruel to show shock, horror, pity or revulsion in front of the injured, especially those who had cried with relief when we arrived. But there was one thing that really turned me

Blood and Bandages

Above: Infantry stretcher bearers walk up Longstop Hill in Tunisia 23rd April 1942 in readiness for the forthcoming battle.

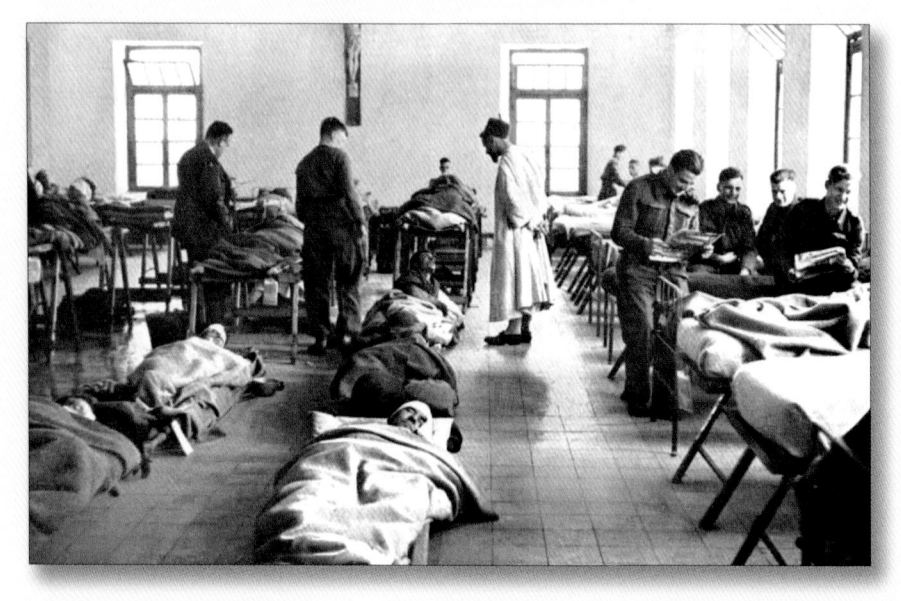

Above: A casualty clearing station accommodating more seriously wounded troops.

58

Chapter 4 Enfidaville

over, trying to remove the tank crews from brewed up (blown up) tanks

The men in the Tank Corps had the worst job of all. The tanks carried their own shells and the men virtually sat on top of them, so when one got hit, the shells exploded underneath them and the tanks went up in flames. Sometimes the man in the turret would get blown out and he'd be ok, but inside was different. Their own cavalry field ambulances generally looked after them but if one wasn't in the area, we would go in and get them. We didn't rush. There was no need, because the injuries sustained by those caught inside the tank were always fatal. We could do nothing to help these burned men, half men really, and the sight of those poor souls was nasty, really, nasty. It was different with the infantry. Their injuries were often less cruel so they had more chance of survival. We fought hard to save them and the quicker we could get them back to the advanced dressing station (ADS) and main dressing station (MDS), the greater the chance they had.

Light ambulances shuttled between the casualty collecting post and the main ADS. If ambulances were not available the nursing orderlies had been trained to improvise. Stretchers, blankets, doors, coats, and firemen's lifts were all duly used to carry the injured.

We had to be very fit and very strong because we had to be able to transport conscious or unconscious men, their full kit and rifle under our own steam. If we had started to carry a man back when it was quiet we couldn't suddenly drop him and take cover if the shelling started up again. We just had to keep going and hope for the best. If we were empty-handed when the shelling started we could drop down and dig a trench as quickly as possible. That's why we always carried a small shovel with our satchel. Self-preservation was drilled into us for if we were killed or injured, who would collect the wounded?

Not only that, 'Medical Officers and men of the RAMC are highly trained technical personnel, and, especially during the later stages of a war, were extremely difficult to replace.'[58] Therefore, if a field ambulance lost too many orderlies, its ability to collect, evacuate and treat the wounded would be compromised. This would fatally damage the brigade's operational capability,

Blood and Bandages

Right: Nursing orderlies prepare to move a stretcher case from an advanced dressing station set amongst the shelter of rock.

(not to mention morale), so the entire infantry brigade would be withdrawn from the line until its' field ambulance was reinforced.

One thing that we didn't expect was the long periods of waiting. We thought that we'd be working constantly during a battle but sometimes we'd be waiting two or three hours for the shelling to die down before we could go back out to do our job. It was incredibly stressful just staring at each other in a trench thinking, am I going to be killed or injured by the next shell? To calm my nerves I'd get out my little cardboard chess set and Frank and I would play a game while we waited. That helped a lot because we'd focus on the next move, not the next shell, and after a few games we'd forget about everything else. In fact, once we were in the middle of a game when we heard a thud nearby. We thought, 'cor, that was a bit close,' but just carried on playing. When the shelling stopped we peeked over the top and there was an unexploded shell about a yard away. We leapt out of that trench and sprinted off as fast as our legs could carry us.

Only short-term exposure to the intensity of the front line was sustainable, so one of A company's sections would spend between 24 to 48 hours at the casualty collecting post, (CCP), before being relieved by other of A company's sections and falling back to the advanced dressing station, (ADS). That section remained there for a day or two before returning to the CCP. This to-ing and fro-ing of A Company's sections would continue for four to five days, until the whole of A company was relieved by B company and withdrawn to the main

Chapter 4 **Enfidaville**

dressing station to rest while B company went forward and started the whole process again.

That's why we never got to know the men in B company too well because when we went back to the MDS they were going forward to replace us at the CCP and ADS.

If there were some walking wounded at the ADS near the end of our shift, we'd walk back with them to the main dressing station. If not, we'd normally get a lift in an ambulance or jeep along with the wounded. As usual, we were still within the range of the Axis artillery but 90 per cent of the time the enemy respected the Red Cross and would stop firing when they saw lots of ambulances on the move. They wouldn't stop if only one ambulance was in transit and sometimes there was so much crossfire they couldn't stop at all so we'd just have to take our chances.

Back at the MDS, we had beds for up to 200 sick and wounded. They had to be looked after and their dressings changed so although we'd gone back to rest, we weren't really resting, we just became ward orderlies.

We could never settle in though because we had to be able to follow our brigade whenever it moved. This meant that we always had to be ready to relocate our patients and pack down the MDS at any time. How much notice we got of a move depended on the circumstances. Sometimes the order came through that we were advancing the next day, but sometimes it was within two hours. Packing up your kit and transferring your patients to another MDS within that time was a challenge. Several times I had to rip Mary's photo down because I had no time to remove the drawing pin.

We'd use lorries and ambulances to move the patients and on one occasion we were preparing an ambulance when we saw three planes coming towards us. The chap with me said, "Oh look," I said, "They're Stukas! DOWN!" We hurled ourselves out of the ambulance and onto the ground just as they started firing. A piece of shrapnel nicked the back of my head, an inch higher and I would have been killed.

61

Blood and Bandages

Despite the heavy enemy resistance around Enfidaville, the Black Cats established a slow advance. The 214th field ambulance followed the infantry in its' usual caterpillar style; the main dressing station moved up to take over the advanced dressing station's position; the ADS moved up to take over the casualty collecting post's position and the CCP advanced to create a fresh post behind the new front line.

On 26th April 1943, the 214th's ADS moved into the old CCP and a new casualty collecting post was opened up on the Enfidaville – Bou Ficha Road, two miles north of Enfidaville.[59] A few days later, the 167th field ambulance finally arrived from Iraq. The 167th infantry brigade joined its sister brigade in action and the two field ambulances began to collaborate. The collecting companies worked together and the 167th inherited the 214th's MDS when the latter advanced with the Queen's.[60]

While the Black Cats remained bogged down in the Enfidaville area, other Eighth Army divisions swept into the northern areas of the bridgehead taking Tunis and Bizerta on the 7th and 8th May respectively. With those in their possession, the Allies were able to surround the Axis troops around Enfidaville.

On 9th May, the 167th's commanding officer was visiting the 214th's new MDS when it came under attack killing both him and his driver.[61] Later the same day, the 167th called upon the 214th to help rescue their brigade's wounded who were stranded in No Man's Land.

We usually got to know about men left in No Man's Land from those that had managed to get back. The information went through the brigade and was then passed onto the field ambulance who would arrange a rescue mission. Once the exact location was identified, a section would be detailed to go and rescue the men.

On this occasion, William's A1 section answered the 167th's call for help.

We were always briefed before a mission about the whereabouts of the casualties, the terrain we'd be covering and whether we needed any special equipment. In this briefing, we were told that a large number of wounded were out there and we were going at night. Night missions were always the most dangerous because no one could see our Red Cross brassards in the dark.

Chapter 4 **Enfidaville**

Therefore, we could easily be mistaken for an infantry raiding party, and the greater the number that went out the more likely it was that we'd be taken for combatants. For that reason, we usually went out in groups of six or eight.

As it was, the 167th called for 18 men, significantly increasing their chances of being spotted and attacked.

This was our first night mission. We knew that every second we were out there we'd be in grave danger so we knew we'd have to protect ourselves by crawling on our bellies and using hand signals to communicate with each other. The thing we dreaded most was being caught in the middle of a counter-attack. If that happened, it was likely that neither us nor our casualties would stand a chance.

The events which occurred during the night mission of 9/10th May near the Bou Ficha Road were recorded in the 214th 's war diary.

'During the search, A1 section bumped into a German patrol, which attacked them with hand grenades and then made off. Sgt Abley rallied the section, (with the exception of Pte J.E Sherwood, Pte H Mustoe, Pte R H Palmer and Pte G K Gillan), and, with the help of some Regimental Stretcher Bearers, continued the search.

After the attack, Ptes Sherwood and Mustoe were together but separated from the section. Nevertheless, they continued according to their original orders and found a wounded soldier of the Ox and Bucks and a Regimental Stretcher Bearer. They attended to the man and the three of them carried him on a stretcher back towards the Regimental Aid Post.

On the way, they were attacked for a second time, and a grenade burst immediately under the stretcher. The Regimental Stretcher Bearer and Pte Mustoe were wounded and Pte Sherwood could not find the stretcher or the original casualty. Pte Mustoe was unconscious and, in Pte Sherwood's judgment, mortally wounded. He did what he could for him, dressed the wounded Regimental Stretcher Bearer and then carried the latter on his back to the Regimental Aid Post – a distance of 1.5 to 2 miles. During the whole of the return journey, there was incessant shell and mortar fire and some sniping.'[62]

When they returned from the mission, Private Sherwood and Sergeant

Abley were recommended for the immediate award of the military medal (MM). Private Mustoe's body was found later the same day.

No words of mine can describe what it's like when there's shelling going on in the distance, and you look round a corner and there's one of your own chaps lying there dead with half his head blown off or a leg gone. We had grown hardened to hideous injuries and the sight of dead and dying men, but it really affected us when it was one of our own.

More than anything else, it would strike you that he had no chance. He had nothing to defend himself with so he couldn't have done anything to save himself. Mustoe's death brought home to us the dangers of what we were doing.

On 10th May, Private Harry Mustoe's comrades buried him where he lay and he was later interred in the Enfidaville war cemetery, the resting place of most of the men who died in the last few months of the North African campaign.

The Axis forces surrendered two days later on the 12th May 1943. The same day, the Allied leaders met in Washington for the Trident Conference. The cracks papered over at the Casablanca Conference resurfaced and there was continued disagreement over whether to extend Allied operations in the Mediterranean or scale them down in favour of the cross-Channel invasion. Despite American misgivings at being sucked into Churchill's 'Mediterranean adventure,'[63] it was agreed that two things had to be done, 'to eliminate Italy [from the war], and occupy the greatest number of German troops.'[64] Italy had 34 divisions in France and the Balkans.[65] If they were out of the war, Germany would have to fill the gap with forces from elsewhere, predominantly the Eastern Front. By continuing its' operations, the Allies would also regain control of the Mediterranean.

The Americans were persuaded to extend operations from Sicily into Italy on the proviso that after Sicily had been captured, seven Allied divisions would be brought back to Britain to prepare for what would become known as Operation Overlord.

While the Allies discussed strategy, the 214th dealt with the aftermath of the first campaign.

Chapter 4 **Enfidaville**

Above: RAMC ambulance convoy cross the desert during the North African Campaign.

Above: RAMC ambulances in convoy across the desert.

Above: A camouflaged casualty collecting post (forward advanced dressing station) in the desert.

Above: Lord Lyons (King George VI), with convalescing British troops during his visit to North Africa on 12th June 1943.

The conflict had only just ended so there were still wounded coming in. Some of the 214th set up a walking wounded collecting post while A company was detailed to take over a German ADS.

Medical men had no enemies and the Germans had kept to the Geneva Convention, so we were quite happy to join their medical unit. Indeed, it was quite emotional when we arrived. We all said hello and shook hands before we got shown around. Their advanced dressing station was much bigger than ours and we set to and worked side-by-side for the next week receiving and treating casualties. We got on very well together. We shared our rations and I tasted sauerkraut for the first time in my life.

Being there made me realise that the normal German soldier was no different from me. Most of them didn't want to go to war. They had their wives and children and sweethearts too but, just like us, they had to do what their government said, whether they liked it or not. They weren't Nazis. They had been ordered to fight for their country, just like we had.

Chapter 4 Enfidaville

Because hostilities had ceased, there were no fresh casualties coming in so after the wounded were treated they were transferred back to the base hospital. With the departure of the last men, the ADS was closed and we returned to our own field ambulances. Ours was resting outside Tripoli.

We camped in bell tents near to the coast. We used to run into the sea naked and we relaxed. We wanted to forget about fighting and enjoy ourselves.

There were four to five men to a tent and we would lie like segments of an orange around the base of the central tent pole which was covered in photographs of our loved ones and film stars. I put two up of Mary and Frank put some up of Majorie. Occasionally our burly gregarious Scottish captain would come in and chat with us. He was super. He loved two things, wearing his kilt in the evenings and drinking whisky. I remember one night, he was chatting with us and he got so drunk that he put his arms around the middle tent pole and swung round and round. He was a big man and spun so fast that he bought the tent down. We all collapsed laughing and he just wandered out. Of course, the sound of the crash brought out an orderly officer and we were all gathered up and dumped in a spare tent for the rest of the night.

We were there in July and the heat was unbearable. An order came out that we must be under cover between the hours of midday and 3.00pm so we used to sit in our tents. If we washed our shirts and put them out to dry, they'd be ready within about 10 minutes. When water was very short we were rationed to one chuggle, (a canvas bottle shaped like a hot water bottle), a day. We were allowed to fill it up with water in the morning and do what we liked with it. We could drink it, make tea with it, wash in it, shave in it or wash our clothes in it. The choice was ours.

Then one day, we were told to polish up and parade because a very special person, a Lord Lyons, was coming to inspect us. We were not happy with it because we had to break off swimming but we all polished up and lined up with our best dress on. When we paraded we discovered that it was actually King George VI with Monty. He had come to inspect the troops, well, he came to thank us really, which was nice.

Blood and Bandages

The victory in North Africa not only boosted moral and bolstered Churchill's position, it also secured the Suez Canal, the vital link to India and the Middle Eastern oilfields. Inexperienced American troops who had been routed during Operation Torch 'learned how to crawl, to walk, then run in Africa'[66] and 130,000 German and 120,000 Italian troops had been captured.[67]

Above: Joint German - British advanced dressing station Enfidaville Tunisia May 1943.

Chapter 4 Enfidaville

In accordance with the Casablanca and Trident Conferences, the Allies prepared for Operation Husky, the invasion of Sicily, and Operation Avalanche, the invasion of Italy. The Black Cats were duly divided up. The 168th brigade remained with the Eighth Army for the invasion of Sicily while the 167th and 169th brigades were assigned to a new formation, the Anglo-American Fifth Army commanded by General Mark Clark.

We were happy to be part of the American Army in Italy because their rations were so much better than ours. They had steak and kidney puddings in their tins, whereas in our rations we had meat and veg in one tin and a few dried biscuits in the other. And it was one tin between two.

We stayed in Tripoli and started training for the landings on Salerno beach. We'd get on to a boat which sailed out as far as it could before coming back again and stopping. That was our cue to leap into the water with full kit and stretcher, wade ashore and run up the beach as quickly as possible. As normal this was accompanied by the sound of our sergeant majors yelling at us to, GET DOWN! LIE DOWN! We had to abandon our stretchers in the end because they slowed us down too much.

Mountain warfare training courses replaced desert warfare training and the unit underwent an internal reorganisation. As part of this, A company became the casualty collecting company. It was equipped to open up two light ADSs and was led by an officer with power to act autonomously. It was included in the first order of march, along with the brigade headquarters, so would be the first to receive news of casualties whereupon one light ADS could be set up to collect the wounded immediately.[68]

Mussolini, (Il Duce), was so concerned with the build-up of Allied forces in the Mediterranean, that he asked Hitler for additional German divisions to be sent to Italy to bolster his own forces. Five German divisions subsequently arrived between mid-May and early June, and were split between Sardinia, Sicily and the Italian mainland.

However, by 20th May, Hitler was more concerned about Mussolini and the political stability of Italy, than the Allied build-up. He was advised that Il Duce was an unpopular leader and pro-British sentiment was spreading among the

Italian bourgeoisie and military. In response, Hitler ordered top secret plans to come into effect if Mussolini were deposed or Italy collapsed, surrendered or joined the Allies. Code-named Operation Achse, the plans covered the German invasion of Italy; the forcible disarmament and neutralisation of the Italian armed forces in Italy and the Balkans; occupation of Italian controlled parts of southern France and the control of key frontiers and passes. Moreover, orders were given for the secret assembly of a new army group in Bavaria ready to move into northern Italy if Operation Achse came into effect. Unaware of such plans, on 17th June, Mussolini asked for two more German divisions to reinforce his country. Three were sent. One was deployed at Salerno, a second to the strategically important airfield at Foggia and the third north of Rome.[69]

On 10th July, the Allies invaded Sicily. Despite initial opposition, the advance was rapid. Now extremely concerned about an imminent Italian collapse, Hitler withdrew five divisions from the Eastern Front to reinforce Sicily and moved the division at Foggia to defend the toe of Italy. Nine days later, Hitler and Mussolini met. Il Duce was 'a shrunken man, physically and psychologically' who refused to listen to the pleas of his chief of general staff to withdraw Italy from the war.[70] Instead, Mussolini asked for more German reinforcements and on 21st July, Hitler dispatched six more German divisions to mainland Italy. Thinking that he had emboldened Mussolini, Hitler temporarily suspended the plans for Operation Achse. The same day, the Allies reached Palermo, Sicily's capital, and were greeted as liberators not enemies.

The fall of Sicily pre-empted Mussolini's demise. On 25th July, he was deposed by Marshal Pietro Badoglio, his long term opponent, arrested and spirited away. Hitler was both surprised and enraged and instantly restarted planning for Operation Achse. Consequently, between 27th July and 2nd September, German divisions and the secret Bavarian Army were moved into their Operation Achse positions in Italy, France, the Balkans and the Brenner Pass, while their divisional commanders studied what they needed to do if Operation Achse was activated.[71]

Meantime, Marshal Badoglio pretended to honour the Tripartite Pact with Germany and Japan while trying to negotiate the country's exit from the war.

Hence, he did not oppose the transfer of German troops onto Italian soil but at the same time tried unsuccessfully to slow their flow and dictate their location. In negotiations with the Allies, Badoglio tried to insist that Italy become neutral but be given the protection of 15 Allied divisions north and south of Rome in the event of German reprisals.[72] The Allies refused. They wanted Italy's unconditional surrender but agreed to provide one division to protect Rome and the Italian government. Terms were finally agreed and on 3rd September 1943, the armistice of Cassibile was signed.

Elsewhere, the Eighth Army had crossed the Straits of Messina and invaded the toe of Italy. Five days later, the Allies announced the armistice with Italy, too soon for Badoglio to prepare the Italian forces. The announcement left him with no choice but to confirm that a deal had been struck with the Allies. Unaware that an invasion force was sailing from Tripoli towards the Bay of Salerno, Badoglio broadcast an order that the Italian military must cease all acts of hostility against Anglo-American forces. Hitler was furious. Within minutes of Badoglio's announcement, code word Operation Achse was transmitted to all 40 strategically placed German divisions. 'It was the signal for the German forces to attack Italian forces in all the war theatres of the Mediterranean.'[73]

In the absence of clear instructions and leadership, the Italian population stood little chance when the Germans attacked. Their former allies rounded on them and demanded that they surrender or collaborate. Resistance, like that in Rome and Naples, was brutally extinguished and the Germans took 650,000 Italian troops prisoner, the majority used as slave labour.[74] The remaining military deserted, escaped, went into hiding, or joined resistance groups except 94,000 soldiers, mainly fascists, who voluntarily joined the German Army.[75] The Italian fleet escaped, but was mauled by daylight bombing and two thirds of the Italian Air Force fell into German hands. Such was the success of Operation Achse, that by 10th September, the German high command announced that, 'the Italian armed forces no longer exist.'[76] Unaware that the Germans had invaded Italy from within, news of the armistice was greeted with jubilation on the Allied troopships heading towards the Gulf of Salerno.

Blood and Bandages

Above: The Eight Army bombard the coast of Sicily before the invasion on 3rd September, 1943.

Above: The Fifth Army assembles off the coast of North Africa on 8th/9th September 1943 for the invasion of the Italian mainland.

5

The invasion of Italy

Enfidaville had been a baptism of fire, so we thought, ah well, we're battle-hardened troops now, we can cope with anything. Then, of course, came Italy.

The Germans had correctly anticipated that the Allies would invade at the Bay of Salerno so when the armistice was announced, reinforcements were immediately dispatched to the area.

We sailed with the Queen's assault troops and arrived at our release position at 1.15am on 9th September and waited offshore. There were 18 of us led by Sergeant Abley and we carried our first aid kits with extra supplies on our backs. We were due to go in at zero hour plus 25 minutes.

As the time approached we sailed forward to get as close as possible to Sugar Beach, our section of the landing area. When we stopped, the ramp crashed down and we immediately came under fire. Major Dougall shouted, 'Go!' and without knowing how deep the water was, we leapt straight in. Luckily, it only came up to our waists, so we surged through the waves and sprinted on to the beach as fast as we could. We had to keep running because there were troops behind us. The moment we cleared the beachhead, Sergeant Abley yelled, "Dig in and wait there until you get the order to move." Frank and I found a little sand dune and dug a slit trench. All around us infantrymen were crashing to the ground, dead or injured. They were only armed with rifles, grenades and machine guns and were no match for the German firepower.

We must have been there for about an hour but eventually we crawled further up the beach and made contact with the rest of the company. There were no regimental aid posts (RAPs) and B company had yet to land with our stretchers and equipment, so we made a makeshift advanced dressing station and waited for the order to move. We could see the number of wounded lying on the beach and some of us got over excited and began shouting about what we would do. I was very nervous too but Frank said quietly in his normal slow drawl, "I think we should do this. If we take it easy, maybe we'll be able to do that." As always his self-confidence reassured me that we could get through this safely.

We had to wait until the navy stopped shelling before we could go out to treat the injured. We relied on the signallers to tell us when and the moment we got the go ahead, Sergeant Abley told us to deal with the wounded we could see. We raced around because we didn't know how long we had until the navy restarted the bombardment.

Sometimes there were six or eight of us helping the injured, other times it was just Frank and I. Those that were conscious were delighted to see us and we gave them some water from their water bottles. Some of the men just needed a bit of help to get up and walking again, if they couldn't because they had a leg wound, we made a tourniquet to stop the bleeding. Every soldier had his own first field dressing tied to his thigh and we used that if the wound wasn't too big. If it was, we ripped up his trousers or improvised with whatever came to hand. The stretchers were landing later so Frank and I would make a chair by linking our wrists together to carry those that couldn't walk. As long as a man could put his arms around us we could get him out of danger. Sometimes, the injured were in such a dangerous spot that we had to get them to a safer place before we could even start treating them. Once we'd done that, we'd leave them there and go and find another casualty. If a man was so seriously wounded that we couldn't move him at all, Sergeant Abley would detail two of us to remain with him until more help arrived.

Meantime, on the adjoining Roger Beach, the 167th field ambulance's assault scale had also landed. Like the 214th, they came under fire immediately but had enough time to unload their MDS equipment before machine-gun fire forced them to scatter and dig slit trenches.[77]

Chapter 5 **The invasion of Italy**

By first light, the 214th's ADS had landed and the collection and evacuation of casualties had been coordinated and B section had arrived at the proposed site for the main dressing station.[78]

We slowly followed the Queen's as it advanced from the beach and created ADSs behind each new front line. We eventually ended up at a farm and Frank and I sheltered in a trench between rows of plum tomatoes and grapes. I said to Frank, "Hey, look at those lovely plum tomatoes." And we feasted on them as we watched the landing craft come in. We saw our first three tanks come off one of the bigger ones and I said, "We've got three tanks!" As soon as they landed, the Germans knocked them out, BANG! BANG! BANG! We only had three and now we had none.

By the end of D-day, hundreds of men had been treated on Sugar Beach. Eleven men had been evacuated to the hospital ship[79] and one of the 214th's nursing orderlies had sustained a gunshot wound to the right buttock.[80] Yet, the German response was not as ferocious as expected and there was some doubt about their resolve to repulse the invasion. All doubts evaporated the next day as 'it was now apparent that the landing was very definitely opposed.'[81] One of the Queen's RAPs was ambushed. An ambulance car was captured and three nursing orderlies from the 214th were reported missing. One of them was later found dead with a gunshot wound to the head. Private Sherwood MM, was shot in the chest and an RASC driver in the leg.[82]

However, the pressure felt by the 214th was negligible compared with that which had been experienced by their sister field ambulance, the 167th. As normal the 167th field ambulance was supporting the 167th infantry. The 8th and 9th Royal Fusiliers (R.F) of the 167th had been ordered to 'proceed direct to Battipaglia as quickly as possible to capture the town and its' heights and to hold all roads and bridges.'[83]

Battipaglia lay approximately 10 miles inland from Roger Beach and on 9th September, 9th R.F entered the town as ordered. At 8.30am the next day, officers from the 167th field ambulance entered the town to find a suitable position for an ADS.[84] They did not return and rumours started to circulate that something had gone badly wrong. The 167th's war diary picks up the story.

75

'10th September 2.10pm Captain Forsyth returned in jeep suffering from shell wound to the right calf and buttocks. He reported as follows: - Lt-Col Brown, Major Porter and himself were in the area of Battipaglia doing a recce for a site for the ADS. They were on the top storey of a house when he looked out of the window and saw a German tank approaching. They all went downstairs and took cover behind the building. The tank however saw them and opened fire wounding Major Porter in the leg, (compound fracture tibia and fibula), and wounding Captain Forsyth. The tank approached close and stopped. Lt-Col Brown spoke to the tank commander and pointed out his Red Cross brassard and went to get a stretcher from one of the jeeps. He brought the stretcher back and he and Captain Forsyth were lifting Major Porter onto it when a second tank opened fire from another direction, killing Lt-Col Brown and wounding Major Porter in the head. Captain Forsyth got into a ditch and crawled away to try to get help for Major Porter. Captain Forsyth was picked up by the Brigade Signals Sergeant and came straight to the MDS stopping only to tell people on the way to try and rescue Major Porter…What had happened to Lt Hobcraft he did not know.'[85]

Although investigations revealed that Battapaglia was surrounded, 45 minutes later an officer arrived from the RAP with a fully loaded ambulance. He had managed to find a way out of Battapaglia but confirmed that the 9th R.F was cut off by the Germans.

With the 167th's senior officers dead or wounded, Major Johnston assumed command. He launched a desperate attempt to rescue Major Porter but was forced back by heavy shelling. That night the 9th R.F's commanding officer ordered the town to be evacuated. They fell back to the outskirts of Battapaglia and were joined by 8th R.F and the Grenadier Guards.[86]

At dawn on 11th September, the situation deteriorated further still. Captain Harling was in command at an 8th R.F regimental aid post. He sent a message back to the 167th's MDS saying that they were, 'unable to cope with the flood of casualties.'[87] Major Johnston went forward with six nursing orderlies and an ambulance but instead of finding casualties, found Captain Harling in a 'very excitable state.'[88]

Chapter 5 **The invasion of Italy**

Above: Royal Engineers check for mines on the landing beaches during the invasion of mainland Italy.

Above: Royal Engineers lay wire matting on the landing beaches to facilitate the unloading of stores.

That happened if you got very tense or nervous. It almost happened to me once when word came through that the Germans had broken the line and were advancing on us. All I could think was, oh God, here come the Germans. We are going to get captured. And when you can hear the rumble of approaching tanks, your mind gets disturbed and in that moment fear gets hold of you.

Captain Harling was relieved and escorted back to the main dressing station to rest. Sometimes a morphine induced sleep was enough to cure those with mental exhaustion. Captain Harling's rest was good enough for him to return to duty eight hours later.

At dusk the same day, reports were received that parts of 8th R.F were retreating under a fierce German attack. In fact, they were retreating in

Above: Nursing orderlies evacuate a wounded man from the front line to the base hospital.

disorder and had to be forced to return to their posts at gunpoint.[89] When Major Johnston went forward to check that the RAP was still operating, he discovered that it had been abandoned and that Captain Harling was missing.

That was very bad. The sergeant should have taken over, but if he didn't and Captain Harling ordered them to abandon the post, the orderlies would have had no choice but to obey.

A few hours later, Captain Harling arrived at the MDS, again in a 'highly excitable state.'[90] The sleep treatment had clearly failed so he was replaced and evacuated.

He would have been sent straight back to the hospital ship.

The prevailing view being that those with psychiatric injuries 'tend to infect other people.'[91]

The German counter-attack at Battapaglia on 10th September slowed the Black Cats advance 'and the division as a whole was virtually sitting on the beaches.'[92] Two more German divisions had also arrived to repulse the landing and the Allies were trapped on the sand dunes, in the nearby tobacco fields and peach orchards. They were also being bombarded with heavy fire. In addition, logistical problems hampered what progress they could make. The naval smoke screen, designed to hide Allied shipping, blanketed the beaches and exacerbated existing problems of beach control. Stores could not be deposited or collected quickly due to traffic congestion around the dumps. There were no cranes to remove heavy equipment from landing craft and driverless vehicles had to be winched off.[93] 'In the first three to four days when the tactical situation was critical and all available fire power was needed, a large tonnage of completely inessential stores were landed e.g battledress, gaiters and caps.'[94]

On 12th September, the Germans launched such an effective counter-attack that General Mark Clark wrote in his diary that, 'the situation is extremely critical.'[95] The next day, the Germans threatened to break through and plans were made to evacuate the troops. Clark appealed for help from the Eighth Army which was advancing rapidly from the toe of Italy because the German forces had been withdrawn to defend Salerno. Their help did not arrive as swiftly as Clark needed. Instead it came from additional naval and bomber support. By 15th September, the bridgehead had been secured and by the time the Eighth Army advanced to within 60 miles of Salerno, the Germans had already begun their slow retreat to the River Volturno. On 17th September, the two Allied armies finally linked up.

Battapaglia had been flattened during the intense Allied bombing but the 167th field ambulance still returned to salvage usable equipment and remove the bodies of their men.[96] The battle of Salerno had cost them 12 officers and 10 other ranks. The 214th's losses were lighter, two dead and four wounded.[97] Overall the Americans had suffered 3,500 killed missing or wounded and the British 5,500.[98]

With the Salerno beaches secured behind them, the Fifth Army began its' advance towards Naples to secure the port, vital to the Allied supply chain. Throughout, they encountered German rearguard actions, minefields, booby traps, and blown bridges. Meantime, the Eighth Army travelled east across Italy to continue its' advance up the Adriatic coast.

The first few miles from Salerno were quite flat and we advanced quite quickly. We stopped in a schoolhouse, a farmhouse and some delightful peach orchards smothered with fruit. First thing in the morning, Frank and I would come out of our tent and admire the beautiful Italian landscape. Mount Vesuvius dominated the distant horizon and it was erupting all the time. It was incredible to see the flames and sparks shooting up, especially at night. Then we started to move into the mountainous areas inland and our advance slowed as the roads became narrower and we ran into bottlenecks.

The Allies had discovered their first natural enemy; the Italian topography. The Apennine mountain range runs like a wide spine down the length of central and southern Italy into Sicily. In its foothills lie east-west flowing rivers. It is a landscape which generously favours the defender, particularly south of Rome. In fact, in 1943, the Allies had invaded a country that was so hostile to aggressors that it had not been captured from the south since AD 536. Even Napolean Bonaparte was credited with saying, 'Italy is a boot. You have to enter it from the top.'[99] Moreover, the moment the armistice had been

Chapter 5 **The invasion of Italy**

Main German defensive lines across Italy 1943 – 1945

announced, the Germans had seized the high ground and started embedding a succession of defensive lines to which they could retreat and hold. They worked furiously for the lines had to be completed before the Allies could reach them. Subsequently, mountain settlements were overwhelmed with slave labour or conscripted locals who blasted out solid rock to build deep underground shelters, machine-gun nests and pillboxes. In the foothills, farms, houses and orchards were razed to the ground to create minefields and killing zones. Each defensive line was intended to slow the Allied advance for long enough to complete the one behind it, most particularly the Gothic Line which protected the route into southern Germany. Even before the Allies had set foot on mainland Italy, they had encountered the immense disadvantage of the Italian terrain. In Sicily, for instance, 60,000 Germans had held off 450,000 Allied troops for 38 days by skillfully using her hills and mountains.[100] The topography also significantly reduced the advantages of mechanized warfare. The Po Valley was the only real tank country and in the mountains there were few paved roads to facilitate the rapid movement of men, supplies and equipment. Instead, there was an abundance of fast flowing rivers, steep winding roads, narrow tracks and paths suitable only for men and mules. Hence, unlike the North African campaign, Italy was principally an infantryman's war which would have to be fought in conditions similar to those of the First World War.

As we trudged north to Naples, we had an army of bedraggled refugees behind us. They had fled to the south when the Germans occupied the north so as we pushed up, they followed. They were friendly and would chat all day long and it made us feel good because we felt we were doing something worthwhile. However, they caused logistical problems because they got in the way. For some men, like George Catchpole, it was heaven. Everywhere he looked there were young Sophia Laurens who hadn't seen chocolate or soap for a long time. We had weekly rations of both and some of the women would do anything for a bar of soap or a bit of chocolate so you could more or less have any of them, every night if you wanted. Frank was horrified by the thought of having any sexual activity with anyone other than his wife. I thought sex was a natural thing and we had been away for over a year, but Frank's influence steadied me so we were very gentlemanly and just chatted to those who knew a little bit of English.

They told us how the Germans had gone into their towns and villages and rounded up the young men to work in their labour camps. Some had managed to escape and were still hiding in mountain caves. One lady said a lot of the Italian girls had given themselves to the Germans to get the rations, but there had also been a lot of rape and torture and not just by the Germans, some of the Allies had done the same. That made us quite angry, but as we were only being told second-hand, we didn't believe everything she said.

I had great sympathy for the refugees because they were in such a poor state. We always tried to give them what medical help we could, but we couldn't use too many dressings or pills because our first priority was to our own men. However, if we thought they really needed help, we did what we could. This happened one night when we were staying in an Italian village. A young man turned up at our billets in a desperate state. His wife had gone into labour and he didn't know what to do. The duty doctor and I followed him to their hideout in a nearby cave. We delivered the baby safely and they were so grateful that they named him after us. I shall always treasure that.

On 1st October, after 22 days of fighting, the Allies entered what was left of Naples. The Germans had wrecked it spitefully as a punishment for resisting their occupation of the country. Aqueducts had been blown up to deprive the Neapolitans of water; libraries, sewers, electricity stations, factories and the port had been ruined; time bombs had been left in major buildings and some dead bodies were booby-trapped. The Black Cats by-passed Naples and by the 5th October, William's A company had followed the Queen's 25 miles further north-east. Under cover of darkness they entered Caserta military hospital. Abandoned inside they found 31 American and 116 British and other Allied prisoners of war.[101]

They were overjoyed to see us. They said, "Two hours ago the Germans suddenly got into lorries and left, but we didn't know what to do. Then we heard tanks and we thought it was them, but it was you!" There were a few medical men amongst them and they said that the Germans had treated them quite well and given them freedom to look after the other prisoners' injuries. From that I assumed that if we were captured, we would just carry on with our Red Cross work.

Once the prisoners of war had been examined and passed back down the line, the 214th's main dressing station moved into the hospital and opened to receive 250 divisional battle casualties.[102] In the event, it treated 380 men but the sick outnumbered the sick wounded. A and B companies were ordered to assist in the main dressing station and check and replenish supplies, supplies which fell woefully short of demand. Their commanding officer, Lieutenant Colonel Richards, recorded that the number of stools and tables should be increased by 500 to 1,000 per cent, and the number of bedpans, urinals, cooking and feeding utensils by 100 per cent.[103]

Blood and Bandages

We spent 10 days camping in the grounds of the magnificent Caserta Palace while the brigade rested and awaited reinforcements. We'd done our bit from Salerno to Naples and we needed to get away from all this fighting and experience normal life again, so when we weren't checking that our equipment was in good working order we'd wander around the vast gardens enjoying the monumental lakes and baroque fountains.

Some days we were given permission to visit Naples and do a bit of sightseeing. The first time Frank and I went, we were struck by the sight of loads of Italians walking around with coats fashioned from British Army blankets. They were obvious because of the colour and the letters, 'WD' for war department, were visible on the hems.

Although Frank didn't do it, the sale of army blankets was rife. We were all given a standard issue of three blankets each but when we went forward to the front line we only took one and left the other two with our kit. If your blankets were gone when you got back, you'd go to the store and the Quartermaster Sergeant would say, "Did you lose any kit when you were away?" and you'd say, "Oh yes, I've come back and someone's taken my blankets." You'd automatically be given another two. They never checked to see if you were lying so you could claim that your blankets were gone even when they weren't and sell the replacements on the black market. They fetched quite a few liras so you could easily live off the proceeds without having to spend your army pay. It was so widespread that towards the end of the war, so few men were drawing their weekly pay that the orderly room said we had to contact them if we wanted it. We knew it was wrong, but we all just saw it as a little bonus from the war office.

With most of the 169th brigade held in reserve at Caserta and Santa Maria, the 167th brigade, supported by 201 Guards brigade, advanced to its next objective, the formation of a bridgehead across the River Volturno. It was 20 miles north-east of Naples and its' capture would create a buffer behind which the Allies' supplies could be safely unloaded at the Neapolitan wharves. It was also the river to which the Germans had retreated after the battle at Salerno.

Chapter 5 **The invasion of Italy**

Above: William in uniform aged 30.

Above: British infantry pass through a Salerno street, September 1943.

That part of the Volturno which flowed through the Black Cats' divisional boundary was described in the 169th infantry brigade's report. 'The Volturno', it said, 'varied in width from over 100 yards to 50 yards. It had a swift current and was only fordable at very few places… and with the rain then falling the river was rising rapidly. The river lay within steep banks which gave an almost vertical drop of 30 feet which made the launching of assault boats impracticable along most of its' length.'[104] In fact, there was only one suitable place from which the crossing could be made. Unfortunately, the report continues, 'it was the most obvious… and was

Chapter 5 **The invasion of Italy**

well covered by German small arms posts and pillboxes and also by his arty and mortar defensive fire... in view of the rise in the river and the strength of the enemy positions on the far side it was not practicable to put an adequate force over by swimming or wading at any other point with a view to their coming around and attacking the defences at the rear.'[105] Nevertheless, the 167th still had to secure the bridgehead and an attack was scheduled to start at 8.50pm on 12th October.[106]

The Germans seemed to know exactly when and where the attack would take place so they launched a pre-emptive strike on the troop concentration area as they formed up. The 167th's report described the subsequent assault, 'in spite of the enemy fire, 7 Oxf and Bucks attempted to form up and advance to the river but in so doing sustained many casualties and had several assault boats damaged... officers recced forward to find alternative approaches to crossing places but reported that the crossing place itself was under such heavy fire that even if the troops reached the bank, a crossing was unlikely to be successful. Finally after several further attempts had been made... permission was asked to stop the operation.'[107] It was granted at 10.19pm. One officer and ten other ranks had been killed and one officer and 45 other ranks wounded.[108] The rest of the Fifth Army had greater success so the corps boundary was re-drawn and part of the 167th and the Guards crossed the river via an American bridge. The 169th infantry brigade and 214th Field Ambulance followed afterwards.

By the last week of October, the bridgehead over the Volturno was secured but, in a pattern that typified the whole campaign, it came at a price. By 31st October 1943, just over 50 per cent of the 2/5th Queen's brigade had been killed, missing or wounded while in the 167th brigade, the 9th Royal Fusiliers had lost 25 out of 35 officers and 547 out of 800 men.[109]

87

By October, winter had also set in and the troops faced a 40 mile advance from the River Volturno to their next objective, the Gustav Line.

The Gustav Line stretched across the narrowest part of Italy from just south of Ortona on the Adriatic coast to the Gulf of Gaeta on the Tyrrhenian coast. This 87 mile long defensive barrier was anchored in the west by the natural fortress of Monte Cassino which overlooked route six, the Fifth Army's only practical road to Rome. As the Gustav Line was still under construction it was imperative that the Allies reached it fast. However, it had become obvious that the Allies had a second natural enemy; the Italian winter. Driving rains, mud rivers, sleet and snow made road and tracks impassible. Heavy armour got bogged down and trapped in narrow roads and the weather reduced the number of aircraft sorties. Worse still was the impact upon the troops described unsparingly by an American war correspondent, 'our troops were living in almost inconceivable misery… thousands of men have not been dry for weeks. Other thousands lay at night in the high mountains with the temperature below freezing… they dug into the stones and slept in little chasms and behind rocks and in half-caves. They lived like men in prehistoric times.'[110] In the absence of effective air cover and heavy armour, it fell to the exhausted infantry to lead the advance often with close quarter fighting with machine-guns, small mortars, grenades and bayonets. Progress inevitably slowed giving the Germans more time to fortify the Gustav Line and surrounding area. They used it most effectively. They blew up bridges across the River Garigliano, laid extensive minefields in the foothills which were themselves defended by machine-and anti-tank guns, built pillboxes in the mountains and concealed their artillery on the reverse of slopes.

The belligerents finally made contact on 2nd November at the River Garigliano. William and Frank were exhausted but within days were in action in one of the Allies most gruelling operations to date.

6

Frank's capture

Contact was made near the Mignano Gap through which the road to Rome, (route six), passed. The gap was guarded on either side by massive mountains both of which were in German hands. From this position, the Germans could rain down artillery on any troop movements below, effectively rendering route six impassable. To advance to Rome, the Allies had to outflank the Mignano Gap by seizing the mountains on either side.

The British X Corps was ordered to take Mount Camino on the southern side of the Mignano Gap, a task that was given to the 169th brigade of the Black Cats. Accordingly, the 214th field ambulance made preparations to evacuate and treat the wounded in the forthcoming assault.

Mount Camino was a 3,100 foot partially vertical formation which the Germans had protected with minefields, booby-traps and heavy weapons. The 169th called its upper reaches bare arse, because 'it was as bare as any desert, no shrub nor vegetation, bare hard rock with crevices large enough to get your foot down.' [111] D-Day for the attack was 5th November 1943.

19-year-old Lieutenant Wheatley of the Grenadier Guards, (Wheatley) took part in the attack and recorded that the 'Platoon Commanders were, as usual, in excellent heart and being frightfully funny, but beneath their bluff they knew a blood-bath was imminent.'[112] Once the minefield had been overcome, a nine and a half hour climb followed. It was up a precarious track, one with which William would later become familiar. Wheatley recalled that, 'all went well until we came over the summit, then everything in hell opened up… the fire was withering… little did we guess what was to follow.'[113]

What followed was a succession of blistering counter-attacks which drove the 169th off any peak that it reached; some companies were surrounded, others were trapped or overrun. The 214th's first stretcher party arrived with the Scots Guards who carried ammunition and more rations. The fighting ceased while the orderlies collected what wounded they could, but half an hour after their departure the fighting restarted. A few days later, another stretcher party arrived but they fared less well than the first. They were attacked on the way down resulting in the death of two nursing orderlies.

The 169th held out for five days, (some by clinging onto near vertical slopes), before the attack was called off. The men tried to conceal their retreat by grimly propping up the deceased, dressing them in steel helmets and pointing their weapons at the enemy. The first battle of Monte Camino left so many casualties that Monte Camino was nicknamed murder mountain.

Following the aborted attack, the order was given for the army to rest. As usual, that did not include the medical corps so the 214th continued to treat the sick and wounded.

We were working in a cave one morning when an officer came in. He asked if anyone was interested in opera because he had some free tickets for the Force of Destiny which was being performed in Naples the next day. That was my cup of tea so I said yes instantly. It wasn't Frank's, he preferred popular music, but he said he'd come along and see what it was like.

Naples was a fair distance away, so after dinner we left the cave and went back to the MDS so we could leave from there. Next morning, I was not feeling too good and some spots had started to appear on my neck but I ignored them and we left at about 8.00am. Two hours later we arrived in Naples.

I wanted to get something nice for Mary so we spent the morning ambling around the shops. I bought her a coral necklace and a brooch for Mother, then we treated ourselves to steak and chips. It tasted totally delicious after the monotony of weeks of rations.

Chapter 6 **Frank's capture**

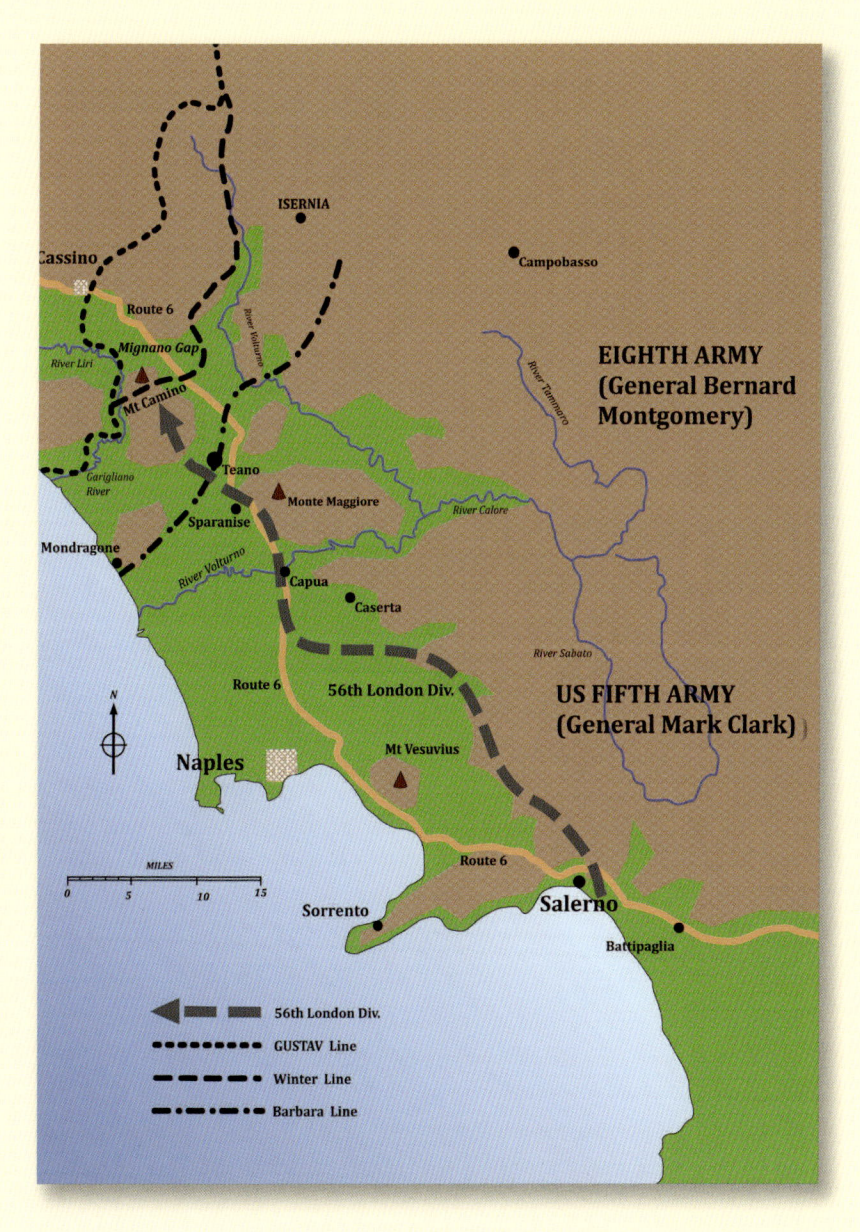

Above: Advance to the Gustav Line September – November 1943.

The performance was in the afternoon so after lunch, we found San Carlo Opera House. It was beautiful and inside there were rows and rows of sumptuous boxes right up to the gallery. As I sank into a chair and was enveloped in the music, I thought what a lovely bright interlude amongst the horrors of war.

The performance lasted about four hours and at the end I asked Frank what he thought of it. He said he had enjoyed it, it was just rather long and he wished that he could have understood what it was about. It was then time to catch the transport back to our main camp.

Next day, Frank and I returned to the cave but by the time we got there I was feeling very odd and more spots had appeared. I reported to the medical officer who ordered me to return to the MDS immediately because I'd got shingles.

When one of our own came in, we tried to make them feel a bit special so when I was admitted I got a few extra painkillers and a few more drinks than the rest.

William's hospital admission coincided with his second wedding anniversary so thoughts of leaving Frank were replaced by those of Mary.

'OUR DAY'

My own dearest beloved Mary,

... Many times today, as I have laid here with our wedding photo by my bed, I have relived every moment of that happy day...For two years now, my darling, we have been married... and our two anniversaries have been celebrated with us many miles away from each other...

I remember, darling, how we used to plan what we would do every anniversary, the party we would have, and the roses I would get you... I do hope and pray... that next year, when 'Our Day' comes again, we shall be together, happy once more and able to celebrate it in the way we have planned to spend it.

On this day again, darling, I vow to you before God and with all my heart, that I shall love and adore you madly forever... I am living only for you

Chapter 6 **Frank's capture**

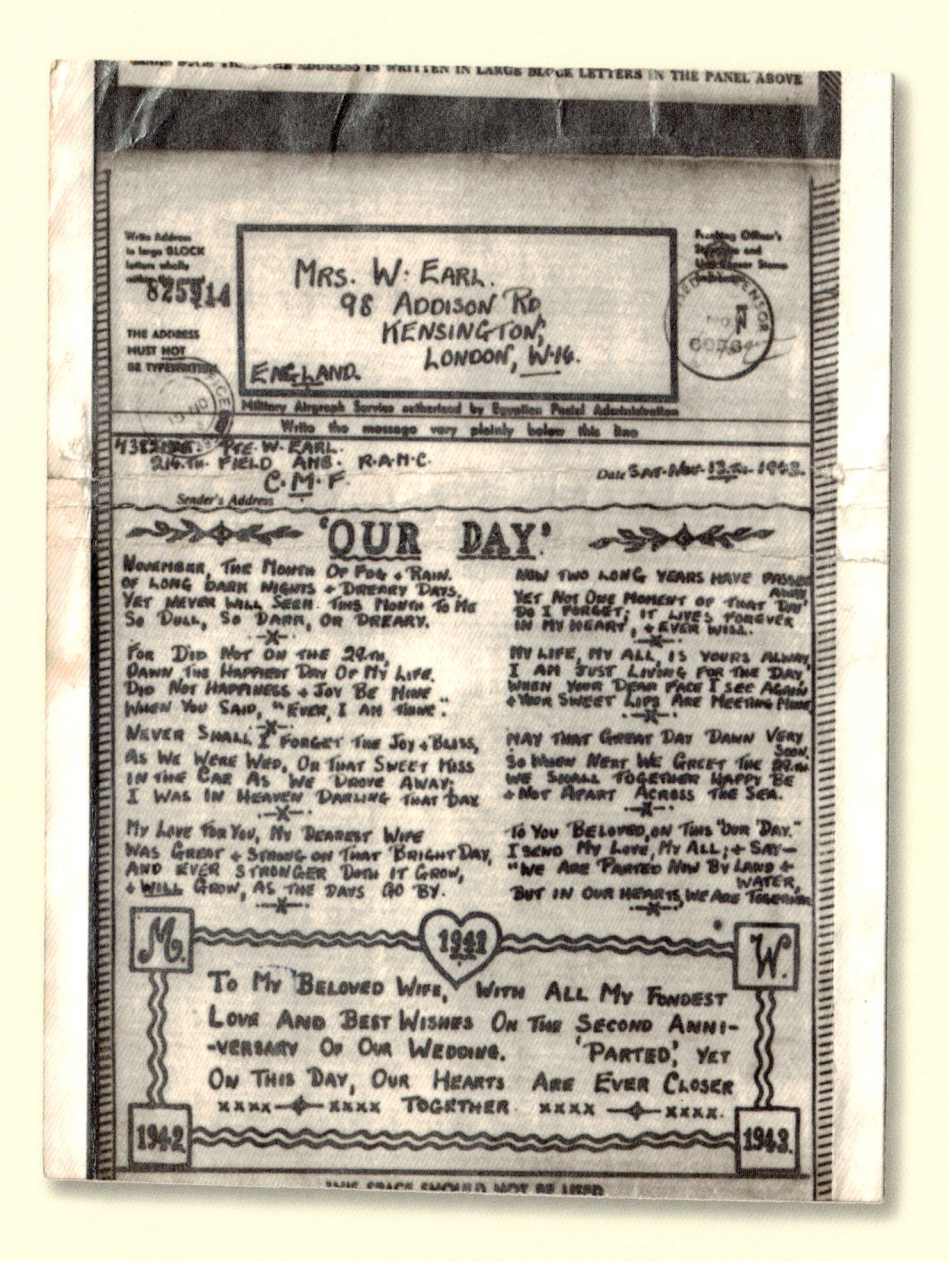

Above: William's lettercard to Mary November 1943 sent from Italy.

Right: A jeep evacuates an injured German soldier down the line.

my dearest wife and may the great and happy day of my return very soon come, so that we can together live and be happy with each other, as is our right.

While William rested at the MDS, on 1st December, the Black Cats secretly moved into position for a second attack on Mount Camino. It began after a huge artillery bombardment which caused one German officer to note that it was 'of an intensity such as I had not witnessed since the big battles of the First World War.'[114]

The Black Cats launched the main assault on 2nd December. The 167th brigade attacked one ridge whilst the 169th took the other. Once again, the casualties were high and the routes down to the ADSs were steep and perilous. The wounded men not only had to contend with their injuries, but also the fear of the downward journey. Indeed, the first patient to arrive at the 167th ADS on 5th December was very badly shaken.[115] By 7th December, 507 more casualties had undergone the same trial before reaching the ADS.[116]

During the assault the 167th field ambulance sustained 11 casualties, one of whom later died from his wounds. However, this time the Allies were victorious and Monte Camino's nickname was changed to million dollar hill to reflect the cost of the Allied bombardment.

After three weeks in hospital, William rejoined his comrades as they harboured in the Cascano area, 17 miles south of Monte Camino. The

Chapter 6 **Frank's capture**

Queen's were now engaged in minor operations but the inclement weather had worsened and it was not long before William's shingles re-emerged.

It was on the 27th December and it was our turn to go forward after a five day rest at the MDS. When we arrived at the advanced dressing station we were told that the infantry had been engaged in a fierce battle and lots of casualties had been left in No Man's Land.

Frank and I were asked to join a 12 man team to rescue them. We were to leave at midnight, but I collapsed three hours before zero hour. I hadn't been feeling good all day but I'd shrugged it off, but when Frank saw me fall he insisted that I went to see the medical officer. I was examined and told I couldn't go on the mission. I tried to argue that Frank and I always worked together, but the M.O wasn't interested. He said, "You know you're not to go. You'd be a weak link. You're to return to the MDS and someone else will take your place." To be described as a weak link was crushing, so I argued no more.

I saw Frank before I left and told him, "I can't come with you. I've tried." He replied, "You've got to be fit because you know what we've got to do. I'll see you when you get back." Then he left to join the other men and I reported to the officer in charge while they found my replacement.

I was sent back to the main dressing station and at midnight they left. None of them returned.

I was recovering well at the MDS when, three or four days later, news came through of what had happened. There had been a counter-attack by the Germans and they'd been caught in the crossfire. That was the one thing we all dreaded so I could imagine their terror when the firing started up.

Six of them were killed instantly, including my replacement, and the other six, Frank amongst them, had been wounded and taken prisoner.

There was an unwritten rule between us and the Germans that if medical men were captured, they would be returned to their own side unless it wasn't possible. It was days since the mission and if they were going to be returned they would have arrived back by now.

95

Instead, Frank was on his way to Moosberg Stalag, a vast prisoner of war camp in Bavaria.[117]

I took it very badly indeed. Not only had my closest friend been captured, my replacement had been killed. The thought that he had died so that I could live upset me deeply and I sunk into depression. The officers could see how affected I was and decided that I needed a mental rest, so although the shingles had almost gone, I was sent to recuperate in an army convalescent home in Sorrento.

I travelled down by truck. When I arrived I was amazed to see this lovely peaceful town with craft shops and bistros. The British Army had taken over two hotels on the hill overlooking the beautiful Bay of Naples and the Isle of Capri. I reported for two weeks of complete rest. When the officer saw me he said, "Ah. You're a medical man. That's just what we need." He could see that I had no physical injuries so he announced, "You'll be on the staff." The Queen Alexandra (QA) nurses were there so I joined them and reverted back to my normal role as a ward orderly.

It was wonderful to work alongside women again and they were such fun. The QA nurses were masters at keeping up moral and once they organised a lovely party for those of us who weren't bedridden. "We tried to get some balloons but couldn't, but there will be balloons there," they said. And they kept their promise. They decorated the ward with lots of blown up condoms. It was great.

I'd usually finished my duties by lunchtime so I'd leave the hospital and mooch around the quaint old streets and piazzas and explore the ornate churches. I generally ended up at a nearby gelateria where I would treat myself to an ice-cream. As I roamed around I wondered what Frank or Mary would have thought of it. I could feel the depression subsiding but I could also sense that the absence of Frank's friendship was leaving a deep and lasting scar.

Every week the medical officer would assess each patient to see if they were fit to return to their unit. He saw me twice and on each occasion I was considered fit but he would not release me until more nursing orderlies came in for treatment and I could be replaced.

Chapter 6 Frank's capture

By this time Mary, David, and Cissie had been bombed out of their home in Shepherd's Bush and the council had rehoused them on the Peabody Estate in Hammersmith. Mary and David now lived alone in a two bedroomed flat in one block and Cissie in a one bedroomed flat in another. Although the place wasn't as nice as Addison Road, I was relieved that they were safe.

In fact, the new living arrangements exposed Mary to unforeseen dangers. She now lived without her mother but with a small child in a strange place without friendly neighbours upon whom she could call for help. This isolation, exacerbated by her natural friendliness, left Mary exposed to the unwelcome advances of some unscrupulous men.

On 11th February, after almost four weeks rest, some orderlies arrived and I was told that I could return to my unit. There was no transport so I hitch hiked my way back and I caught up with them on the Garigliano Front.

By the time William rejoined his comrades they had crossed the swollen River Garigliano in a 'big and costly attack' and had gained possession of some of the forward positions of the Gustav Line.[118]

I was pleased to be back. The lads wanted to know how I was, how did I get on with the nurses and did I have any of them. All normal army banter.

Whereas William was rested, the divisional commander, Major General Gerald Templer, reported that, 'after two weeks of bitter fighting the Black Cats were weary and much below strength… and it was firmly believed by all ranks that we were now due to come out of the line for a period of rest and recreation.'[119]

Then all of a sudden we were told that we were being pulled back to Naples. All they said was that we were to join an invasion force further up the coast.

In fact, they were heading to the terror that was unfolding on the Anzio beachhead.

Blood and Bandages

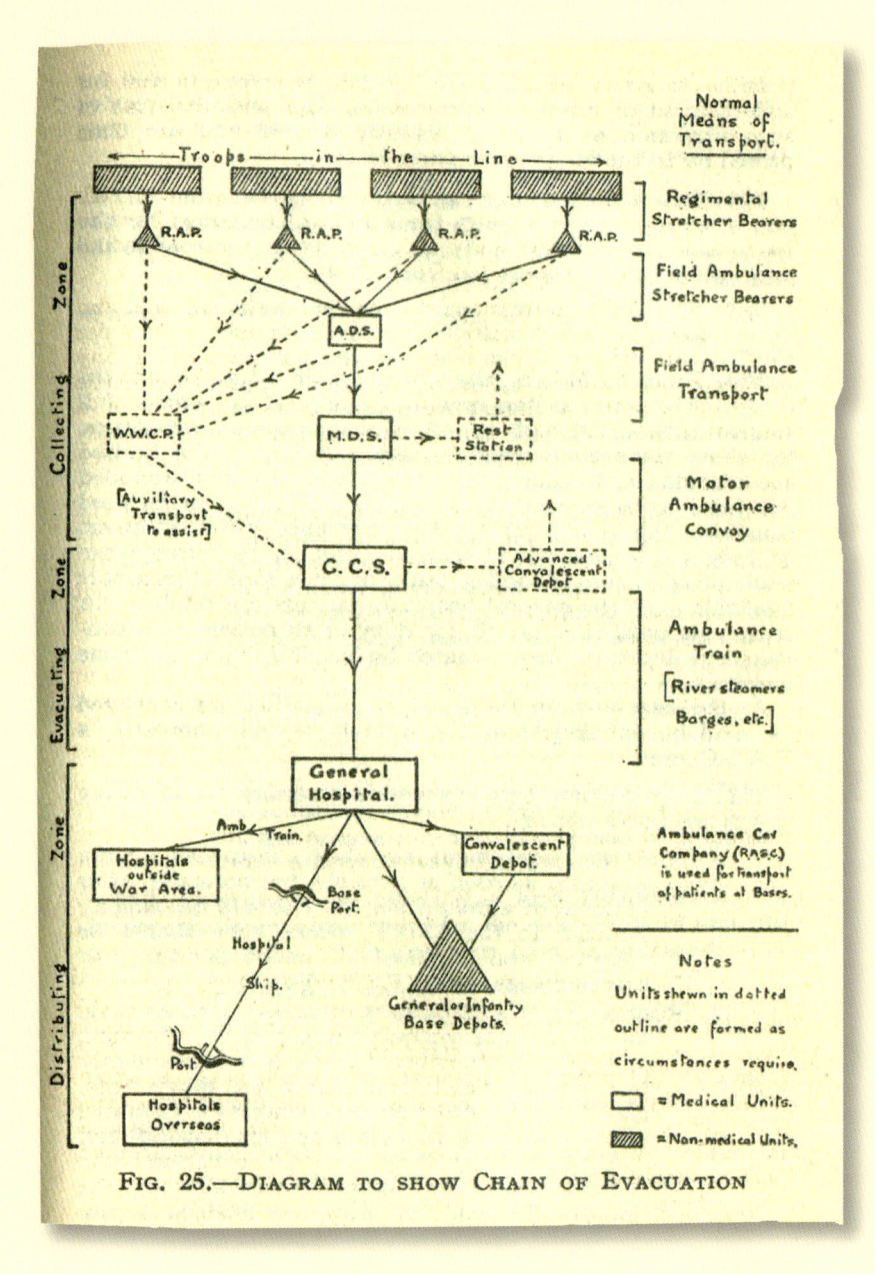

FIG. 25.—DIAGRAM TO SHOW CHAIN OF EVACUATION

Above: RAMC Training Manual 1935. *(courtest of the AMS Museum Aldershot)*

7

Anzio

Taking the Gustav Line had proved much harder than expected and the Allied advance had started to stagnate. In order to breathe new energy into it, it was decided that there would be a surprise amphibious attack at Anzio, 60 miles north of the Gustav Line. The intention was to outflank the Germans forcing them to withdraw from the Gustav Line, thereby relieving the stalemate.

Code-named Operation Shingle, the landings at Anzio and Nettuno were set for the 22nd January 1943. They caught the Germans completely by surprise and were a total success. By the end of D-Day, the German garrison of 1,180 troops had been completely overwhelmed by 36,000 Allied troops and 3,000 vehicles.[120]

Commanding the Allies was US Major General John P Lucas, a naturally cautious man who had been warned by his superior, General Mark Clark, to build up the bridgehead carefully before advancing. Lucas did, but without any apparent sense of urgency despite being urged to advance more quickly. While he dallied, 'Case Richard,' the German code for an amphibious attack on the Anzio area, was signalled triggering a mass mobilization of troops into the area from all over Italy, France and Yugoslavia. By the end of January, the 76,400 Allied troops on the bridgehead were being watched by 100,000 German troops positioned in the surrounding Alban Hills.[121] The American Nazi propagandist, Axis Sally, (Mildred Gillars) described the scene on the bridgehead as 'the largest self-supporting prisoner of war camp in the world.'[123]

The subsequent Allied attempts to advance were ruthlessly repulsed. On 3rd February, the Germans launched their counter-attack with one intention, to annihilate the Allies or drive them back into the sea. The Germans had placed a noose around the Allies' necks and had started to tighten it.

The Black Cats' divisional commander, Major General Gerald Templer, (Templer), set the scene in his report on Anzio. 'The British and American forces in the beachhead found themselves, after suffering heavy casualties, forced to retreat slowly before this ever-increasing pressure...it was to hold and if possible to restore this gradually deteriorating position that our Division was rushed to Anzio.'[124]

Hence, the Black Cats left the Garigliano Front in secret, one brigade at a time and went straight into the front line upon their arrival. The last to leave was the 169th, arriving in Anzio on 17th February.

Their sector of the front line was on the left-hand side of the beachhead. The area facing the Germans was in a section of raised ground cut with a profusion of gullies, to the south of this was the important lateral road which ran east-west and crossed the main Anzio-Carrocetello road at the flyover, below that was a section of woods and meadows.

Within 24 hours of their arrival, 2/7th Queen's received orders to relieve a stricken regiment. Unfortunately, due to faulty intelligence, the relief coincided with a German offensive to eradicate the latter. In the ensuing five day battle of Carrocetello, 2/7th Queen's was virtually wiped out and precious ground was lost.[125]

By the end of their first week on the bridgehead, the Germans had made a total advance of about 1,000 yards into the Black Cats' position. Templer noted, 'the situation from our point of view...did not give us great grounds for confidence...it was resolved that not another yard should be given away.[126] Meantime, William's collecting company contended with their own difficulties.

The only cover we had was in little gullies and we were finally able to establish a casualty collecting post in one of these. It was trench warfare up there and the CCP was under constant threat but luckily the Germans never actually hit it.

The gullies were key positions for the collection and evacuation of casualties, but their topography was far from ideal as Templer described; 'Each

Chapter 7 **Anzio**

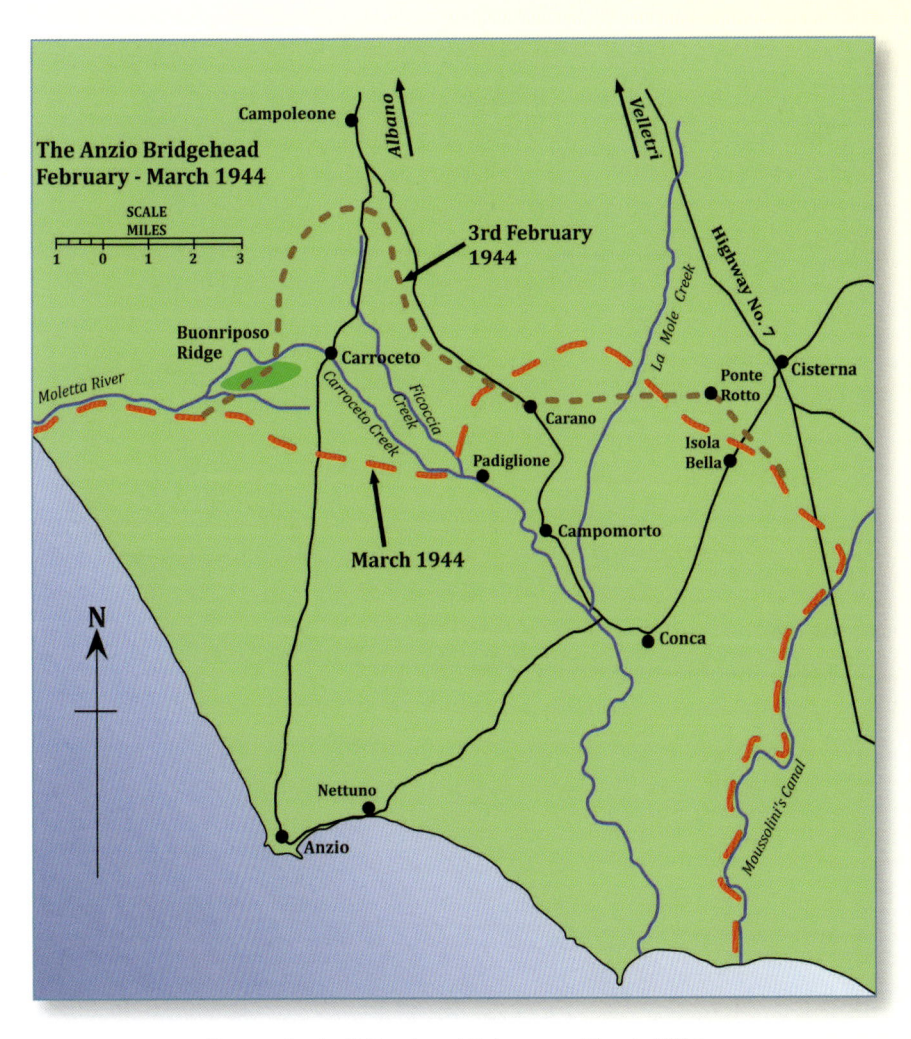

Above: Anzio Bridgehead February – March 1944.

was some 60 to 70 feet deep and 100 to 150 feet wide. These gullies usually had small streams flowing through them and their steep muddy sides were over-grown with thick bushes and small trees. They formed an intricate maze of hidden approaches…and whilst travelling through them on foot it was the easiest thing in the world to get completely lost. A great deal of confused and very bitter fighting took place in the bottom of these gullies.'[127]

The fighting was intense and nasty. There were few lulls during which we could collect the wounded, so it was agreed that twice a day, once in the morning after the night fighting, and once in the evening before it got dark, two orderlies would stand up in the gully and hold up a great big Red Cross. They'd stay like that until the Germans noticed and stopped shelling. That was our cue to rush out and collect the injured. When we got them all back to the CCP, the flag would be lowered and the shelling would start again.

Collecting the wounded was one problem, but evacuating them was another. It was so muddy that we couldn't get our ambulances up to the CCP to collect them. Luckily the American jeeps could travel over any ground so we adapted them to carry stretchers on each side. Once I went back with an English officer on one side and a German officer on the other. The route was treacherous so we took it in turns to drive back to the ADS. I was lucky not to be hit but a lot of our men weren't and were killed or injured on the way.

Hardly surprising, for the route was along a slow and boggy track known as Artillery Lane. Templer explained, 'It passed right through the centre of our gun areas and the heavy shelling it received combined with the unwanted weight of traffic made… progress along it…daily slower and more uncertain.'[128]

With Frank gone, I didn't have a chess partner, so I couldn't play to help calm my nerves. By that time, I was so battle-hardened that I almost didn't need it. I just crouched there quietly ready to brace myself against whatever was coming my way.

There was one occasion when the firing stopped and we were told to go through the German front line to collect our wounded. Normally the German medical men would have taken our wounded so we assumed that they must have been having the same trouble with transport as we were. It was risky to cross the line.

Indeed, at that time the Allies had reported several instances of the Germans abusing the white flag, Red Cross and stretcher bearers, by using

Chapter 7 **Anzio**

Above: A nursing orderly provides 'comforts' to wounded soldiers.

them to cover the withdrawal of troops under fire or spy on Allied positions. It had reached such proportions that in some sectors commanders were prohibited from agreeing a truce to collect the dead or wounded. Others had started taking supposed 'stretcher bearers' prisoner.

We were RAMC men and were only interested in the casualties, but there was always the chance that we could inadvertently glance down and see something we shouldn't. As we clawed our way up the gully into No Man's Land the Sergeant yelled, "When you get there, don't look down! Don't look down!" When we passed through the German front line we ignored everyone, even the friendly ones and we didn't make eye contact. We just shut ourselves off, collected our wounded and took them back as quickly as we could because at any moment they could accuse us of spying and take us prisoner.

The whole situation was terrifying and we were angry. We'd heard rumours that on the day after they'd first landed, two officers drove a jeep to Rome with no opposition. Rome was a sheltered city. Once there we would have been ok. We blamed the Americans for their decision not to advance and kept on asking each other, why didn't they go forward when they could? We felt that if only they had not waited days to build up the bridgehead, we could have advanced to Rome before the Germans had had time to move in their divisions.

Such a view was widespread and, coupled with the strain of the constant bombardment, was too much for some of William's comrades. Two men in A company who were already on a charge for refusing to go back to the CCP, defied a second order to return.[129]

When our comrades' mental health became too unsafe for them to continue, they'd normally be sent away from the front line to nurse at the base hospitals. That gave them a chance to recover. That wasn't possible at Anzio so they stayed on the front line getting worse and worse. Some were even shell-shocked.

However, the situation deteriorated further still as the Germans tightened the noose with relentless counter-attacks.

We eventually lost that gully and were forced to retreat further back.

Templer continues '…the total area of ground lost in the last month was causing our arrangements behind the actual front line to become more and more cramped. We had virtually only one practicable gun area, … and this, shared alike by Divisional and Army Group artillery, soon became uncomfortably crowded. In a defensive battle of this sort, the gunners of course are kept busy day and night and the enemy soon had all our gun positions pinpointed. Thus, day by day, hostile shelling of this area grew more and more menacing, both in intensity and accuracy… The various echelon and administration units had to be crammed into the narrow strip between here and the sea and thus they collected their fair share of the 'overs' which had been meant for the gunners. In fact the whole bridge-head was becoming a decidedly unhealthy spot.'[130]

Our CCP and advanced dressing station (ADS) had been pushed back towards the main dressing station (MDS) on the beach and we became dangerously intermingled with the fighting troops. Almost every second men were being killed or injured all around us and it was a terrible strain. Being jammed together like that also created many more casualties because any shell would find not one, but a group of infantrymen. Despite the great big Red Cross on the ground, the MDS was subject to air attacks because of our proximity to the infantry. The only way we could protect ourselves was to try to lie low as much as we could during the day and do what we could with the wounded we had. It was mostly at night that we were able to move about freely and collect the freshly wounded.

By 25th February, the 167th infantry brigade was operating at 35% of its normal capacity, 168th brigade at 50 per cent, and the 169th at 45 per cent, except 2/7th Queen's, which was down to 15 per cent of its normal strength following the disastrous battle of Carrocetello. Templer recorded that the 'actual numerical strengths had fallen well below the danger limit…there could be no avoiding the fact that the bleak prospect before us included a very real possibility of a German break-through and a last desperate 'back-to-the-sea' stand on our part; and plans to cope with this were now made. … the Divisional order that all lines and localities would be defended to the last man and the last round was taken quite literally by all ranks. The spirit in the beachhead at this time was a grim and defiant one.' [131]

At one point, I could look over my shoulder and see the sea. We thought we were facing another Dunkirk. We'd lost about half our men by this time and there were occasions when I had to collect one of them either dead, dying or very seriously injured. The few of us that were uninjured were working almost non-stop, day and night, and there was nowhere to rest because there were no safe areas. Burying the dead became a luxury.

The Germans attempted to breakthrough at the end of February 1944. They were beaten off and made their last important counter-attack on March 2nd. German gains were quickly retaken but Templer commented that 'contact with the enemy was still close and keen and the position remained distinctly critical and unpleasant.'[132]

The pressure on the Black Cats was finally lifted a week later when command of their section of the line passed to the British 5th division and they left Anzio for Naples. In an unprecedented move, the 214th left its' vehicles and equipment at the beachhead for its' successor, the 141th field ambulance.

Below: Stretcher cases arrive at the base hospital in Nicastro.

Chapter 7 **Anzio**

During their 18 days on the bridgehead the 214th had suffered appalling losses.

We lost half our men at Anzio and when we finally got onboard our troopship, we just held onto the rails and said, 'C'mon get us out of here. Please, please, start the engines and get us away from this hell hole.' There was a great shout of relief when we drew away from the shore. I don't know how, but somehow we had managed to survive.

Staff Sergeant Ross Carter Duffiel of the American 504th parachute regiment, a veteran of the bridgehead, wrote later that any man that fought at Anzio had it 'seared into his brain like a burn with a blowtorch.'[133]

He was right. Anzio was possibly the most terrifying and dangerous battle that we were ever involved in and the memory of surviving second by second was impossible to forget.

After a short journey across the Tyrrhenian Sea, the traumatised men disembarked at Pozzuli. They moved rapidly onto a staging camp near Naples, before reaching their final destination at Sarno where baths were organised and filthy uniforms were exchanged for new. The next day, all but essential ranks were given a day off duty.[134]

We realised how lucky we had been to survive and how grateful we should be that we were still alive.

The 214th collected the 141th field ambulance's vehicles and equipment before commencing its journey through Potenza's snow-covered mountains to Gravina.

Despite their traumatised and depleted state, the 214th was still operational so on 20th March it opened an MDS to treat minor sicknesses.[135] It remained open for four days before the division was taken out of the line for a 'period of rest, reinforcement and training.'[136]

107

Blood and Bandages

8

The price of friendship

While the German stranglehold dragged on, the 214th embarked on MS Batory bound for British occupied Egypt.

The accommodation was very good and within a day of their departure, the officers were treated to a cinema show while the other ranks watched a concert.[137] However, it was just window dressing.

Call it exhaustion, stress, trauma or whatever you like we were never quite the same after Anzio. For 18 days we had lived with the constant fear of being killed or captured and it showed on our faces. I found myself getting more annoyed with people than I used to and I desperately missed Frank's calming influence to bring me back to an even keel.

Not surprisingly, William retreated into his own world and focused on Mary's 23rd birthday.

31st March 1944
My own dearest beloved Mary,
…Now darling as the end of your birthday is drawing near I feel I must write a few lines to you … only on 2 of your birthdays were we together, your 19th and 21st. The latter one is well remembered darling as we were together at Ipswich enjoying that wonderful life of happiness that was ours … last year darling I was many miles away from you and this year finds me in exactly the same position… My dearest… How I have longed today to see

Left: Sheet of proofs of Mary and David March 1944.

your dear face again, to kiss your tender lips and hold you tight in my arms; yet it seems I must wait and wait each day being harder to live without you.

O darling, I am getting so tired of it all yet I do carry on somehow knowing that the day will come when I shall return home to you. I pray darling that it will very shortly come, it is all I am living for ... At the moment we are enjoying a nice journey on the sea... It has, thank goodness, been nice and quiet and the weather is warm and fairly calm... we are also quite comfortable having a good bed to sleep upon and the food is also quite good... Since we got settled in all we have been doing is resting, reading, talking and doing a little washing. ... I often spend hours just looking at the waves and thinking of you darling and how I long to be with you...

All the boys are well, but wish like me we were on our way home...I still miss Frank a lot but I expect I shall get used to it in time... I do hope you are keeping fit and well and also dear David...May God bless and keep you safe always. All my love and all I possess, yours alone, always and forever love and kisses to dear David. Your own ever-loving Husband Will.

His letter crossed with Mary's which was written on the back of a sheet of photo proofs. Just as William hid the horrors of Anzio, Mary hid the vulnerable position in which she found herself on the Peabody Estate.

March 23rd 1944.
Thurs.
Well my darling here is our son David. I wonder what you will think of him. They were taken on Feb 4th 1944 when he was 1 yr. and 9 months old... When I took him I had to wake him up very early and of course he was tired darling. As you will notice in the first few shots he looks very bored. The man had a monkey on his hand but David couldn't make it out, hence the bewildered expression and open mouth. Then he got so bored he put his little thumb in his mouth. Actually darling I was very pleased about this, as you will be able to visualise him doing it. He still does it and I call him a baby boy.

Of course, later on, the man started throwing things at him and actually

Chapter 8 **The price of friendship**

Left: William in Egypt March 1944.

got him to laugh and as you will see he is almost curled up with laughing in one. Of course darling the 2 end rows spoil the entire thing with my face in it... I didn't go prepared for a photo and as you know these are the bare proofs. I was going to edit the last 2 lines out but Mother said you would like to see them... I must say he is just like you my darling and I'm sure you will agree. All I am waiting for now is the day when you will see him in the flesh and be able to see his sweet little ways and his saucy ones, be able to play with him and have fun with him while he bathes. Let us hope and pray it will be very soon.

David sends all his love.

All my love darling, you ever-loving wife Mary xx

The 214th docked at Port Said in Egypt on a fine morning on 2nd April, and marched to the railway station for an immediate departure to Qassasin Camp. The 70 mile journey to the tented desert camp took two days but after setting up, all ranks, including the commanding officer, were given four days' leave in Cairo.[138]

Cairo lay 50 miles south-west of Qassasin and sprawled along the River Nile. This was a mythological city of flat roofs and feluccas, palm trees and pyramids, muezzins and minarets. Bronzed servicemen clad in hats and shorts mingled with women in flowing jalabiyas and men in long white galabeyas. The wide elegant boulevards seemed to cock-a-snoop at the narrow backstreets full of swerving bikes and caleches. On the River Nile, feluccas glided silently, their elegant sails filled by a warm breeze. William was in the land of the Pharoahs, and it insisted on nothing, but his full attention.

But without Frank I didn't feel so confident. I felt lonely and lost. I needed friendship, so I turned to some of the men that I'd trained with in Kent. Men like George Catchpole. Some were still just interested in smoking, drinking and girls but they were the only ones I could be really friendly with so I joined their group. They were alright, but not like Frank at all. We went on tours to the historic sites, like the great tombs and Luxor. We'd go to drinking holes and watch the girls dancing around. Frank and I used to keep ourselves to ourselves so it all seemed a little bit foreign to me.

On 25th April, the unit moved north to Cowley camp at Mena, a huge tented and hutted military camp dwarfed by its neighbour, the great pyramid of Cheops.[139]

We used to play football against the 167th field ambulance, the RASC, and some of the Queen's right in front of the pyramid. They were pretty competitive. In one game there was a corner, and as I leapt up to catch the ball, the opponent's centre forward barrelled into me knocking me out and breaking a rib.

The weather was very hot but beautiful and in the evenings, when the training was over and it had cooled down a bit, the sergeants would rig up a makeshift screen and show us some old films. There were several showings because there were so many of us. Locals used to come to watch too and once one of them leaned his bike against the screen and the whole thing collapsed. That didn't go down well.

Sometimes we were allowed out to see the Cairo nightlife. We'd gather at the famous Shepheard's Hotel, buy Egyptian beer and sit on the warm terrace watching the girls saunter past. After we'd had a few drinks and felt quite merry, George would lead us off to these exhibitions where we'd watch strippers, belly dancers and girls who did unbelievable things to empty beer bottles! I was still adapting to life after Frank so it made my hair stand on end. It was great fun, yet exhausting, to watch all those poses.

After the show, the girls would flirt and you could invite them to join you. You couldn't touch them, but you could buy them a very, very expensive drink.

Meantime, senior officers reflected candidly on the preceeding six months of operations.

Divisional intelligence noted that the Italians were natural informers, 'at the [River] Volturno and again at the [River] Garigliano, local engineers were discovered and interrogated… but…makeshift methods not only fail to get all the information available but …involve treating the local population in a way quite fitting to a defeated enemy but not to a liberated ally.'[140]

Despite the empathy shown at Anzio, Major General Templer complained of the army process from recruitment through to active service. He wrote, 'had we in Italy battalions of the skill of the parachute battalions, we should have done very much better. The main faults are failure to give the infantry the pick of the recruits, inferior training before drafting to fighting battalions, and keeping battalions in the line for too long between re-fitting and re-training periods.'[141] The 168th's brigadier also thought the problem lay with training and reported, 'we have not in our basic training, paid sufficient attention to good rifle and shooting. This has been born out by the lamentably low standard of marksmanship amongst the infantry soldiers and their disinclination to shoot… the value of good rifle firing was learned in 1914…but unfortunately the weapon training pundits during the interim periods between the wars forgot the value of ordinary straight forward shooting and went in for 'fancy' range practices.' The brigadier was also vexed by the over reliance on the bren machine gun and grenade and the inappropriate calls for defensive fire which resulted in, 'a false picture… of the real state of affairs at the front.' He criticised junior leaders for acting predictably and the men for being 'hypnotised by the crest of a dominating height.'[142] The brigadier of the 169th was no less critical, particularly of the impact of reinforcements joining platoons. He noted that, 'the platoon is a team and should function as such… this sudden introduction of strange new officers, NCOs and men directly before or during a period of fighting …encourages desertion through lack of confidence … in their leaders, and causes casualties.'[143] All agreed that the lack of fresh troops had been responsible for turning some of their victories into partial successes and that fresh reserves were crucial.   Yet at that very moment seven divisions, promised to Operation Overlord at the Trident Conference in 1942, were leaving Italy in support of Operation Dragoon, the invasion of southern France. Amongst them were the notorious mountain troops, the Goums.

While the senior officers reflected in Egypt, the Gustav Line was breached, and the Allies finally broke out of the Anzio bridgehead. However at Anzio, General Mark Clark, in breach of orders, had changed direction and marched into Rome on 5th June. In so doing, he failed to cut off the German Tenth Army's retreat from the Gustav Line enabling them to retreat to the Gothic Line. More importantly, Operation Overlord, (the invasion of France), and Operation Bagration, (the Soviet attack on the German Central Army Group) had commenced.

Operation Overlord started first. In anticipation of the amphibious attack, American and British paratroopers had landed in Normandy in the early hours of 6th June 1944, (D-Day). At 4.55am, the troops landed on five beaches. By the end of the day, 150,000 Allied troops had managed to get ashore and establish four sizeable beachheads.[144] The Allies immediately embarked on the battle of Normandy with the intention of reaching Paris within 90 days. As anticipated, Hitler moved troops from the Eastern Front to reinforce his troops in Normandy. On 22nd June, the Red Army launched Operation Bagration at Belorussia in the east. It was the 'largest and most thoroughly prepared operation of the war so far.' It attacked on four fronts with 2.4 million troops, 5,200 self-propelled guns and tanks and 5,300 aircraft.[145] The spectacular return to France dominated newspapers and newsreels at home and in the public's mind no other D-Day mattered.

The bitter slow slog of the Italian campaign could not compete with the speed and excitement of the Normandy landings and after 6th June, the war in Italy was relegated to a backwater, a position from which it has never recovered.

Chapter 8 **The price of friendship**

Above: Nursing orderlies help a wounded German soldier to the ADS.

By 10th July, the Black Cats had been re-equipped, reinforced and retrained so they left Egypt and returned to Italy. The 214th disembarked at Taranto Port and headed for Tivoli camp, 20 miles east of Rome where they were issued with day passes to Rome.[146]

We had survived Anzio and there was this general feeling of, 'now we can really live so let's have wine, women and song.'

I got every third day off and on my free day would leap on one of the lorries that collected us from camp and dropped us off in central Rome to do some sight-seeing.

One morning, I went along to see the Papal audience for serving personnel. That was such a moving experience and one I shall never forget. I watched the Pope get carried in on his gestorial chair. The catholics went forward and kissed the Papal ring, then after he'd gone, we all walked off to see the Sistine Chapel and the other vatican treasures. I'd missed classical music so when the chance came up, I went to the Rome Opera House to see the famous baritone, Tito Gobbi, in Tosca.

Whenever the men rested, measures were put in place to prevent them catching sexually transmitted diseases.

A couple of little rooms were set aside and we would give the soldiers a couple of condoms before they left for the eternal city. When they returned we'd hand them little tubes of mercury anointment and some permanganate of potash to wash themselves out. If a man caught a venereal disease he was instantly taken out of action and treated as if he was wounded. As this effected the strength of a unit anyone diagnosed with VD was put on a charge.

The Forum was where the prostitutes hung out. All you had to do was wander through the ruins and you'd find one, or you could go with one of the young boys who met the army lorries yelling "Sorella! Sorella!" and tried to pull you off somewhere to enjoy the charms of their 'sisters.' A lot of men lived out their sexual fantasies or had sex whenever they wanted, all for a bar of chocolate, cigarettes or a tablet of soap.

Sex was easy to come by because so many Italian women had fallen into prostitution to feed themselves or their families. In fact, there was one time when I accompanied George, who was about to go off on his own with a young lad who had promised to take him to a woman. We followed the boy and he took us to a house. Inside was a married woman with her husband sitting at the table and a one-year-old baby in a cot in the corner. They fell silent when we arrived. The woman took George to the bedroom and they

Chapter 8 **The price of friendship**

Above: William and George Catchpole Rome August 1944.

had sex. Meantime, I talked to the woman's husband. It was uncomfortable sitting there trying to make polite conversation while that was going on, but I didn't want to leave George alone in a strange place.

On another occasion, George and I went into Rome. We had a look at a lot of the classical Roman ruins and afterwards we went wandering around. Eventually we found ourselves walking down a rather quiet street. All of a sudden we heard a clink, and there on the pavement in front of us was a bunch of keys. We looked up at this old building and on the balcony was this wonderful female dressed only in an unfastened dressing gown looking down at us and showing off her feminine charms. If Frank had been with me, he'd have said, "We'll just take the keys back and that's it," but I was with George. I looked at him and said, "Well, we can't both go up there." Suddenly another lovely lady appeared on the balcony and George announced joyfully, "The problem has been solved! There are two and we are two, so come on." I hesitated a bit, but he said, "Come on, let's enjoy ourselves." So I said, "Ok." We had a lovely time chatting about Rome and art with these attractive, intelligent and classy women. After a while one of them said, "Gentlemen, would you like to have a glass of wine before or after?" That was our cue to pair off and disappear behind closed doors.

I don't care if somebody says you shouldn't have done that you were married, you had a wife and son. I always say possibly one in a hundred, one in a thousand men, was faithful to their girlfriend or wife at home. We were fit young men and we could be killed at any moment so conventional morals were forgotten, and we enjoyed what happiness we could whilst we were still alive.

The Italian men took a different view. They didn't like us very much because they thought that we were always after their women.

Also, it was not always consensual sex.

The Goums, (specialist mountain troops from the French colonies of Morocco and Tunisia), had an appalling reputation. They raped women and girls (and occasionally old men), wherever they went. Gang rape was common and an intelligence officer wrote that, 'it is reported to be normal for two Moroccans to assault a woman simultaneously, one having normal sexual intercourse while the other commits sodomy… at Ceccano the British have been forced to build a guarded camp to protect the Italian women.'[147] While General Commander-in-Chief, Harold Alexander, personally intervened to stop the abuses,[148] some Italian men took the matter into their own hands. In one village they enticed five Goums into a house with the offer of sex. When they arrived, they were paralysed with poison and while still fully conscious were castrated before being beheaded.[149] The 214th never came into contact with the Goums but did visit the infantry when the division rested.

The foot and tank regiments hadn't got doctors so whenever we rested our doctors used to visit each one and hold sick parades. They would need one nursing orderly to accompany them and it was the sort of job that would be given to a sportsman.

By a stroke of good luck, I had worked as a medical orderly with Captain J.E Elliott from time to time and he asked if I could accompany him on the

Chapter 8 The price of friendship

sick parades. It was like going on a camping trip. We drove out of the bustle of the main unit into the beautiful solitude of the countryside, just me with the captain and his driver/batman for company. When we arrived at the regiment, we pitched our tents, the captain had one to himself and his driver and I shared the other. First thing in the morning the following day, those that had reported sick would go on parade. Captain Elliott would stop in front of each one and assess them. We'd often be tipped off in advance about malingerers and they usually got normal duties in double quick time. Others would be sent for treatment, get light duties or medicine with duties.

Captain Elliott was 10 years older than me and was quite friendly. He'd ask me questions like, was I married? Where did I live? and so on. He was acutely aware of his officer status so he came across as a bit aloof. In fact, he was a very kind man who assumed a fatherly role towards other ranks like me. We got quite friendly after a time and it turned out that he lived in Kensington. I was still with him when I received a letter from my Mother. She told me that Mary was in trouble.

I was stunned. I confided the news in Captain Elliott and I told him that this was inconceivable because Mary and I were deeply in love. I did however fear that someone could try to take advantage of her warm and loving nature. She'd already written to explain that she'd had to ask a relative to stop visiting her for that very reason. The captain listened sympathetically and offered to get to the bottom of it when he was next in England. Not for the last time was I immensely grateful to him.

Then, all of a sudden, on 6th August, the Black Cats were ordered to rejoin the British Eighth Army who had been advancing up Italy's Adriatic coast.

I was happy to be back under English command. I hated General Mark Clark for the part he played in Anzio and held him responsible for holding back the advance and causing thousands of deaths. I couldn't wait to be rid of the man. All he was interested in was getting his photograph taken.

The Black Cats left the Fifth Army on the Mediterranean coast and crossed Italy to meet the Eighth Army, who were in the midst of preparations for the final push, the crossing of the Gothic Line and on into northern Italy.

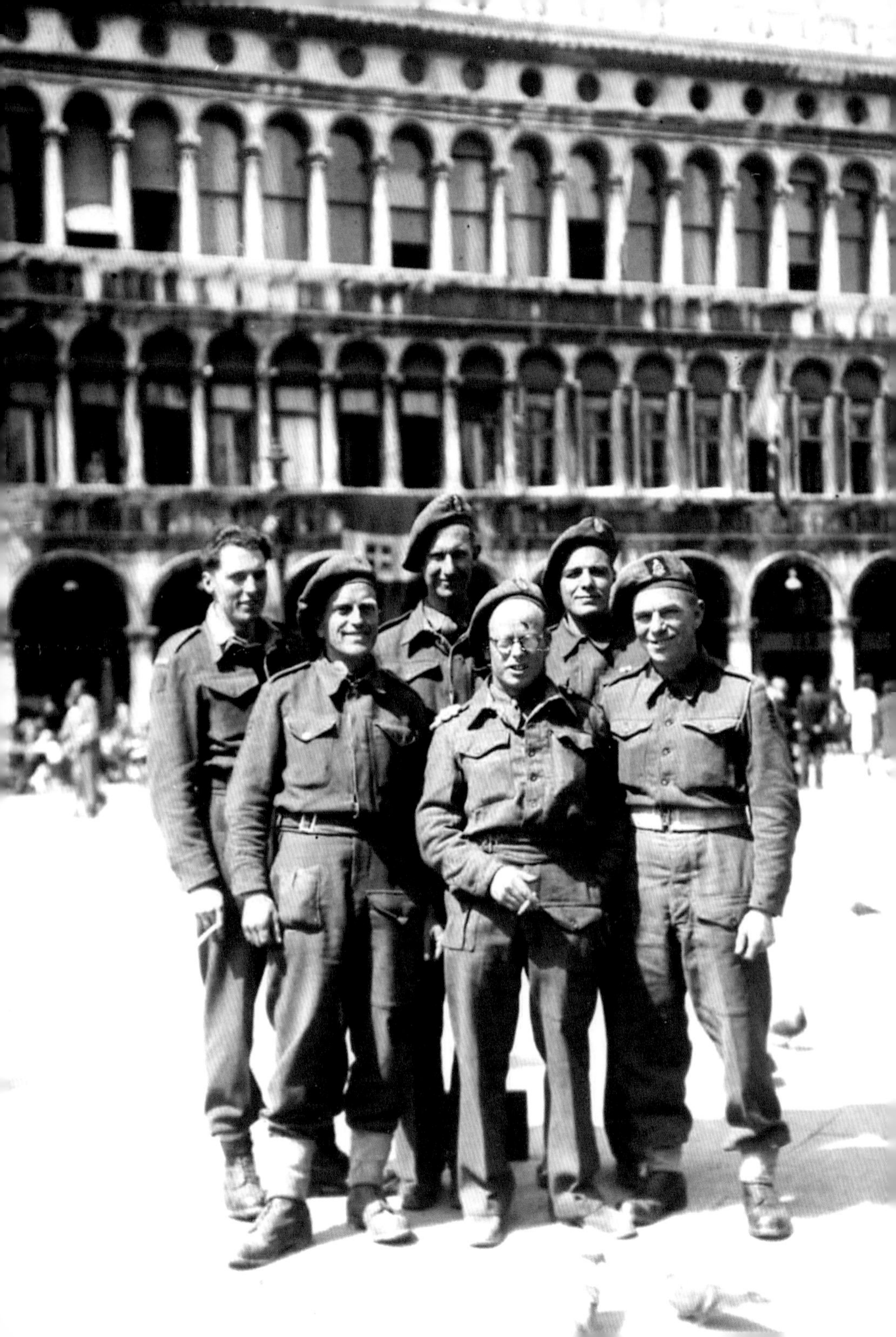

9

D-Day Dodgers

The Gothic Line was the final defensive line up the spine of Italy. It guarded the industrial and agricultural wealth of the Romagna and Po Valley and prevented access to airfields from which the Allies could bomb southern Germany. It straddled the northern Apennine mountains from the Ligurian Sea to the Adriatic and Hitler believed that this 140 mile long, 50 mile deep mountain barrier was impregnable. As with the other defensive lines, the Gothic Line had been embedded with machine-gun posts, anti-tank, mortar and assault gun positions, deep minefields, anti-tank ditches and barbed wire.

It was still under construction when the Allies advanced on its' foothills. They wanted to burst through before it was completed, hence the Black Cats swift departure from Rome. On its way towards the Adriatic coast, the division paused at Petragnano where the commander of the Eighth Army, Lieutenant–General, Sir Oliver Leese, lectured the brigade commanders on the forthcoming operation.[150] Morale was high. 'At last, it seemed, the final push in Italy was near. Non-stop to the Po was a phrase increasingly heard.'[151]

The Allies planned to attack the Gothic Line on two fronts, the centre and the right flank. The Fifth Army would undertake the former and the Eighth, the latter. Secrecy was vital.

The Eighth Army's attack was schedule for 25th August, and as D-Day

Left: William (back row right) and comrades in St Mark's Square Venice May 1945.

approached, the 214th were forbidden to leave their billets unless on duty or speak to civilians. All camouflage and concealment also had to be completed by dawn.[152]

The planned assault covered a 30 mile front and as troops moved up to the start line they beheld the extent of the challenge ahead. One officer noted that, 'When we looked down on, and across the River Foglia to Monte Gridolfo, it must be confessed the situation looked anything but pleasant...all houses had been razed to the ground, trees and vines felled, and avenues prepared between extensive minefields for the hail of machine-gun fire... the assault across the River Foglia and up the bare slopes beyond appeared suicidal.'[153] However, the attack caught the Germans by surprise and the line was breached over a 15 mile front before the 2/5th and 2/6th Queen's had even gone into action.

The Queen's were due to advance on D-Day plus one. On 26th August, William's A company was put on six hours notice to advance with the Queen's leading battalion.[154] Despite the successful Allied attack, the Germans still retained the high ground in strength and had 'a plentiful supply of ammunition, excellent observation and an almost perfect gun area in the foothills of the Apennines.'[155] Subsequently, the moment the Queen's advanced to take Mondaino they encountered hard fighting and casualties were heavy. William and his comrades accepted the risk of being injured by shell and mortar fire themselves as they evacuated the wounded from the regimental aid posts to the two roadside advanced dressing stations.

The next day, the Queen's were driven back by a counter-attack. Two days later, 2/5th and 2/6th Queen's returned to B echelon to rest as 2/7th Queen's came forward. Their rest was interrupted by a bombing raid which killed 12 and wounded 200.[156] It was a costly start to the battle, but the price was not as high as that demanded by their next objective, the Gemmano Ridge.

This mile long, 1,500 foot high ridge had four main heights. 'From these heights, looking down at almost every move of their advancing enemies,

Chapter 9 **D-Day Dodgers**

nearly 3,000 Germans troops waited for the British Infantry to attack.'[157] The Queen's advanced on 6th September but after five days of intense fighting only the eastern end of the ridge had been won.

These two opening battles on the Gothic Line had led to the admission of 1002 casualties to the 214th's divisional dressing station, most with very severe wounds.[158] This figure was virtually triple that which had resulted from the 'battle of the Salerno beaches, the bitterly contested crossing of the River Volturno and the grim fight for Monte Camino.'[159] Unfortunately, such high losses were constantly repeated because during their 26 day advance through the Gothic Line, the Black Cats left flank was open and occupied by Germans. During that time, more enemy artillery rained down on them than in any other action they had seen during the entire campaign. Their losses were crippling.

Mary hadn't written since I'd received Mother's news and I was missing her letters terribly. I'd also started to feel numb with the shock of seeing what war did to a perfectly healthy young man. I felt more and more numb as time went on. We all did, until one day I got really angry.

I was assigned to one of our doctors at an advanced dressing station with another nursing orderly. We were in a little valley and had two tents, A and B. We had been told that the troops were engaged in skirmishes and only to expect one or two injured. The doctor therefore decided that A tent would be for the more seriously injured and B tent for the walking wounded. We waited for the stretcher bearers to arrive with the injured but we were shocked when they did. There were many more casualties than we'd expected and their injuries were serious. Some had arms or legs blown off, others had their chests sliced open with blood pumping out, a few were unconscious. When the doctor saw the state of them, he turned to us and said quietly, "I'm re-designating the tents. B tent for those we can save. A tent for those we can't. If you have time, give those in A tent a drink of water and make them as comfortable as you can." He set about examining each one and in those terrible moments I looked at the poor soldier and thought, will it be A tent or B tent? I'd pray, please let it be B. Then the

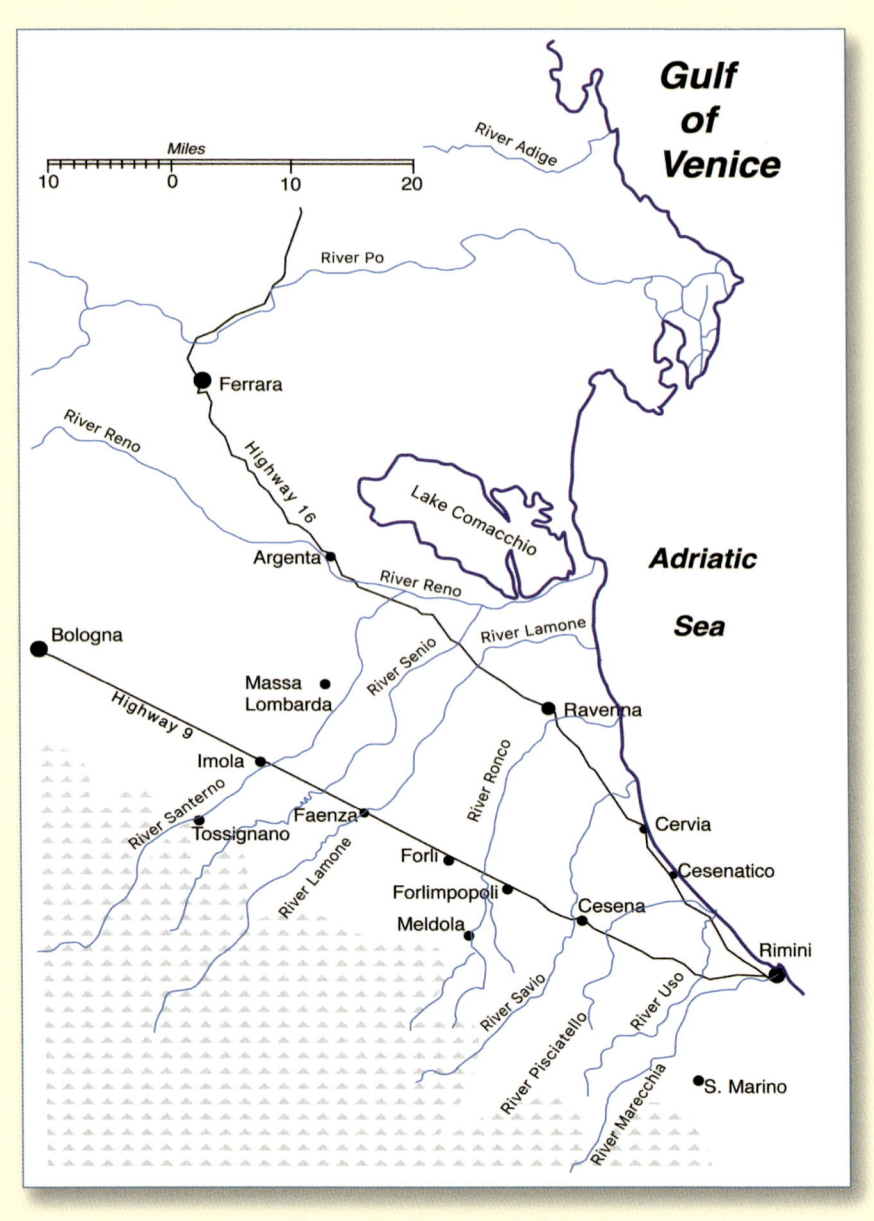

Above: The Romagna in Italy.

doctor would put up his finger and say which one it was. If it was A tent, I would look at the soldier lying there looking so relieved and I'd think, little do you know. I felt as if I was an executioner. This went on until all the wounded had been divided into A and B tents.

The men in the A tent were carried in and left as those in the B tent had to take priority. The doctor did all he possibly could for those men, and jeeps were constantly coming forward to take them back to the MDS for further treatment. Once things calmed down, I'd go back to the A tent and give the men some water and make them as comfortable as I could. If I had time, I would bandage some of them up but then I'd hear a shout outside announcing that the next batch of wounded had arrived and I'd run out and we'd go through the whole process again.

At first, it wouldn't have been obvious to those in the A tent that they had been left to die, but it would become clearer as time went on for we had no time to remove a body or wrap it up in a blanket. It would just be left and a dead body creates its' own atmosphere which grows if its left. Some of the men in the A tent were conscious enough to realise that they were surrounded by the dead and dying. I tried to comfort them as much as I could but I felt so helpless when I knew nothing could be done. I kept on thinking, why are these young men, our friends, our fellow soldiers, our fellow human beings being killed? For what? What would their mothers or their fathers or their wives think of this? What would Mary feel if it was me lying there? It made me feel more and more angry. I felt like bursting out of that tent and screaming up to God, What are You doing? Why are You allowing this to continue? Just stop this! I was only there for a day then reinforcements arrived and it was out of my hands.

After the battle was over, my comrades went to bury those men. They sewed them into their blankets, took their details from their identity discs, buried them and gave their location to the sergeant. The information was sent back to England and after the war was over they were dug up and planted in a war cemetery.

That was a terrible day and one I will never forget.

Fourteen thousand Eighth Army men were killed, missing or wounded during the 30 mile advance through the Gothic Line.[160] The Black Cats were one of the divisions that bore the brunt of the losses. The 167th infantry brigade's casualties were so great that the brigade had to be reconstituted. Indeed, the division's overall effectiveness was so seriously compromised that they could only play a minor role from then on until the start of the spring offensive in 1945. On 11th October, the 214th was duely withdrawn from the line. It rested at Macerata where it opened up a 200 bed hospital. [161]

The other Eighth Army divisions were also depleted but they had to maintain the pressure to assist the Fifth Army's push on the centre of the Gothic Line. 'Throughout the army there was a heroic intensity of effort that discounted weakness and would not admit to weariness and with no pause in the fighting the advance continued and the cold and diminished Brigades entered with gloomy but obdurate hearts, upon the long protracted Battle of the Rivers,' in the Romagna.[162]

The Romagna was split into five areas; a narrow coastal strip of sand dunes and pine woods, behind that lay a belt of reclaimed swamp land kept drained with pumps, next was a central section which was liable to heavy flooding, then came a well-drained and drier Highway 16 and finally the Apennine foothills. The whole area was intersected with 13 major rivers which coursed through steep valleys or 40 foot high flood banks and numerous lesser watercourses which were contained in canals. Only two main roads, including Highway 16, crossed this watery landscape. By the time it was reached by the Allies, autumn was fairly advanced and heavy rains had transformed the Romagna. 'Water was now the main obstacle to the Eighth Army advance rather than high ground.' [163] Streams had become raging torrents; roads had become rivers or reduced to mudslides. Vehicles skidded and collided on greasy surfaces; landslips and broken down vehicles caused roadblocks; supplies, like covered accommodation, hospitals, warm clothing and hard standing could not get through. By early October, two further problems surfaced, the departure of troops committed to other theatres of war and a crippling lack of ammunition and spares as northern France took priority.

Chapter 9 **D-Day Dodgers**

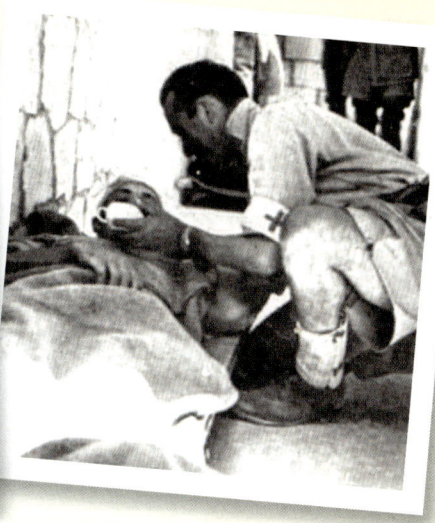

Above left: A medical officer treats a minor injury.
Above right: A wounded man receives a drink from a nursing orderly.

I spoke to a gunner who told me that he only had three shells a day to fire so he used to fire them in the morning so he could have the rest of the day off.

Not surprisingly, by early October 1944, the Eighth Army's advance had stalled. The Fifth Army followed suit a few weeks later and General Mark Clark later wrote, 'after all the effort that had been expended, after all the casualties we had suffered, it seemed almost impossible to give up the idea of completing the breakthrough that autumn…at the end of October, a definite date was set for the renewal of both the Fifth and Eighth Army attacks towards Bologna, but we never kept the date.'[164] Instead, both armies hunkered down to face the one thing they had desperately hoped to avoid, another winter in the mountains.

Their lack of progress drew unfavourable comparisons with the rapid advances elsewhere. In the west, Operation Dragoon had seen the Allies sweep up through southern France; the battle of Normandy had led to the liberation of Paris; Brussels and Luxembourg had been freed and the Allies were in German territory. In the east, the Soviets had swept the Germans back to Yugoslavia, whereas, in Italy the Allies had not even reached the River Po. Conservative MP, Viscountess Nancy Astor, (allegedly) suggested that the Eighth Army were deliberately dragging their heels because they were trying to 'dodge D-Day.' It was an outrageous and unfounded slur and the Eighth Army's sarcastic response was immortalised in the *Ballad of the D-Day Dodgers*.

But even that insult was knocked into a cocked-hat when I received a letter from Captain Elliott. I hadn't seen him since we had done the sick parades together but he had been as good as his word and had visited Mary twice when he was on leave. To him, Mary had confided what had happened and he in turn told me. No-one, other than him, Cissi and I knew the truth but people had been jumping to conclusions to the detriment of Mary's reputation. It was heartbreaking when Captain Elliott passed on Mary's apologies for not having written. She told him that she didn't know what to say to me. It was terribly distressing to read the letter and my first instinct was to rush home to comfort my poor sweet wife. Captain Elliott wisely anticipated my feelings and, unknown to me, had asked for me to be given a compassionate posting to England upon the cessation of hostilities. Yet again, I was extremely grateful to him.

Meantime, the exhausted and under resourced Eighth Army eventually halted north of Ravenna on the River Senio line ready for the spring offensive.

By this time, we hadn't been home for two and a half years. We were constantly asking, 'How long are we going to be struck here?' 'How long will it be before I get home?' 'How long before I see my girlfriend or wife?' All these unanswered questions made us feel frustrated and nudged some of us off the rails. Morals were lowered, and some men behaved in ways they wouldn't have done in normal life, but the prevailing attitude was, 'why shouldn't I enjoy myself? There's a war on,' as if that excused everything. I heard that one group of men had gone into a café and demanded the best but refused to pay for it. Some in my group did lots of things I didn't agree with when we had time off. They'd try and get drunk or have sex. Once, six of us were in a village. We were quite hungry and spotted a smallholding with some

Chapter 9 **D-Day Dodgers**

Above: William (third from left) and comrades resting in Macerata November 1944.

pigs and other animals. There was a cook in the group and he said, "Wouldn't it be lovely to have a piece of pork?" Of course it would've, so some of them hurdled over the fence and jumped into the pen to steal a pig. The middle-aged owner came bursting out of his house to fight them off but they said, "C'mon. You've got lots of pigs, you won't miss one little one." He was having none of it but he was no match for a group of soldiers. We ran off with the pig and ate it later. It tasted delicious.

Over the winter months of 1944-45 the Eighth Army was reinforced, re-supplied, and re-equipped. By spring 1945, the Soviet Army was less than 40 miles from Berlin and the Germans knew they were defeated. However, they would not surrender and the Allied spring offensive in Italy had one simple aim, to bring the conflict to an end.

D-Day Dodgers

Sung to the tune of 'Lili Marlene'

We're the D-Day Dodgers,
 here in Italy
Drinking all the vino,
 always on a spree
We didn't land with Eisenhower
And so they think we're just a shower
For we're the D-Day Dodgers
Out here in Italy

Above: The reality of the Italian Campaign was a bitter fight in conditions that the song's gallows humour only hints at.

We landed in Salerno, a holiday with pay
Jerry brought the band out to cheer us on our way
Showed us the sights and gave us tea
We all sang songs, the beer was free
To welcome D-Day Dodgers
To sunny Italy

Salerno and Cassino, were taken in our stride
We didn't go to fight there, we went there for the ride
Anzio and Sangro were just names
We only went to look for dames
The artful D-Day Dodgers
Out here in Italy

We stayed a week in Florence, polished off the wine
Then thumbed our way to Rimini, through the Gothic Line
Soon to Bologna we will go
When Jerry's gone across the Po
For we're the D-Day Dodgers
The lads that D-Day dodged

Chapter 9 D-Day Dodgers

Once we heard a rumour we were going home
Back to dear old Blighty, never more to roam
Then someone said in France you'll fight
We answered: "No, we'll just sit tight!"
For we're the D-Day Dodgers
The lads that D-Day dodged

When the war is over and we've done our bit
Climbing over mountains, through mud and sleet and…
Then we will all be sent out east
Till B.L.A. have been released
For we're the D-Day Dodgers,
Out here in Italy

Dearest Lady Astor, you think you're mighty hot
Standing on the platform, talking tommyrot
Dear England's sweetheart and her pride
We think your mouth's too bleedin' wide
From all the D-Day Dodgers
In sunny Italy

If you look around the mountains
    in the mud and rain
You'll find scattered crosses, some
    which bear no name
Heartbreak and toil and suffering gone
The boys beneath them slumber on
For they're the D-Day Dodgers
Who stayed in Italy [165]

Left: Artillery men at the bitterly contested R. Volturno.

D-Day was set for 9th April but in a preliminary operation, the Black Cats were ordered to launch a waterborne attack across Lake Comacchio using a new secret weapon, the fantail.[166] The fantail was a sherman tank adapted for amphibious assault. The 214th had commenced training in its use at the end of March. Four were needed to carry the 30 men and stretcher jeeps required for an ADS and they were used to evacuate the wounded on their return flight.[167]

This new secret weapon not only caught the Germans by surprise, it also denied them the natural advantages of the marshy ground and man-made floods which had been protecting their flanks. Equipped with fantails, the Black Cats were able to repeatedly outflank the Germans to the east and west of their positions while tanks advanced along the top of flood banks, tracks, roads, and Highway 16. Therefore, in contrast to the autumn campaign, the spring offensive was rapid and was punctuated by the surrender of large numbers of German soldiers. Even so, extensive minefields could still slow the Allied advance.

In previous quarterly reports the Royal Engineers had identified that the first 200 yards of a track leading to and from a main road were particularly prone to minefields.[168] In the Romagna there were only two main roads both of which were fed by minor roads and tracks. The Queen's were advancing along one such road when their progress was suddenly halted.

Some infantrymen had strayed into a minefield.

Once it was cleared by the Royal Engineers, four of us were detailed to go in and recover the dead bodies. We were told, "Don't bring stretchers. Don't bring any kit. Just bring sacks." We knew then that it would be grim. We climbed into the back of the lorry and tried to hide our feelings by chatting and laughing, but we stopped when we arrived and saw the minefield. My mind could barely comprehend what I was looking at. It looked like a butcher's shop. I saw one man who, an hour or so earlier, had probably been smiling and talking to his pals. He'd probably got a sweetheart or a wife at home but now this man had been reduced to body parts. His arm had been blown across one side of the road, his leg was lying on the other with his boot still on and bits of clothing hung off the rest of his body. I looked at him and I

Chapter 9 **D-Day Dodgers**

thought, why should anybody, any human being be subjected to the horror of being blown apart and the indignity of being scattered about? This was the savagery of war and it turned me inside out. Very religious comrades, men who wouldn't even swear, let rip with the most filthy language I could imagine when they looked at the scene. We had to crush our feelings and get on with our work. So we turned into automatons and systematically worked our way through the minefield picking up the body parts and searching for dog tags. We felt physically sick by the time we had finished. We loaded the sacks onto the lorry and, in silence, brought them back with us. When we arrived back at camp we tried to put the men back together again then we buried them. We couldn't even talk about it later because we did not know the words to explain how we felt, so we just let ourselves feel numb and hoped that we'd eventually get over it. I never did.

Thankfully the war was nearing its conclusion.

On the 19th April, the 214th war diary records that, 'the battle is moving forward very quickly.'[169] Two days later, the 169th infantry was on the banks of the River Po and the enemy's retreat in front of their lines 'had taken on the appearance of a rout.'[170] They were unaware that further upstream the remnants of the German Army were desperately trying to flee to safety across the River Po. Deprived of transport by effective Allied bombing, it had requisitioned carts and wagons to speed its escape but when its' cleverly concealed pontoon bridges were also bombed, all hope faded. By 23rd April, the Americans had crossed the Po further upstream. The German Army was now trapped but it still refused to surrender. With echoes of Anzio, the Allies launched a ferocious attack on the stranded army from the morning of 23rd April until the small hours of the 25th. When the sun rose it revealed, 'a scene of extraordinary desolation and fearful carnage. There was no longer any coherent resistance and along the river lay the ruins of the German Army.'[171]

Unaware of this development, the Black Cats expected their attempt to cross the Po to be resisted. A company was ordered to accompany the forward troops and arrangements were made for a light section to cross with the 2/6th Queen's in DUKWs and fantails.[172] The infantry crossing

Above: 214th field ambulance officers, warrant officers, sergeants and guests' dinner Macerata, November 1944.

commenced at 6.00pm on the 25th April and William's company followed just after midnight.[173] In view of the events earlier in the day the crossing was virtually unopposed and the Black Cats continued their advance to the River Adige and on to Padua. There were pockets of resistance on the way but the German Army in Italy had been neutralised and on 29th April it finally offered its unconditional, but unofficial, surrender.

We knew it was more or less over in the last two weeks, so it was just a case of when they would give up. Each day we wondered, will it be today? As it turned out the news came through when we were with the 2/5th Queen's. "It's all over boys! Peace is declared," announced the sergeant, but just as we'd started to celebrate, an officer burst in and said, "Word's come through that the New Zealanders are racing to be the first to Venice. The Queen's have got orders to beat them and we're going too." We bundled up our kit and leapt on one of their vehicles.

Chapter 9 D-Day Dodgers

As we raced through the villages the Italians came out to greet us. They were cheering, throwing flowers and holding up bottles of wine and ham for us to grab as we flew passed. They wanted us to stop to celebrate with them and once or twice we did, but our objective was to get to Venice first. We finally arrived at 5.00pm, beating the New Zealanders by 30 minutes. St Mark's Square was completely deserted at first then this Italian man came out and tried to sell us some nylon stockings. I bought some for Mary. We were all so excited and happy. We posed for photographs and drank while we waited for the rest of the 214th to turn up. They took much longer to arrive because they lingered on their way and kept stopping to celebrate with the villagers.

Our field ambulance was billeted in Venice for a day then the high and mighty commanders arrived and an order was given that Venice was for the top brass only. They turfed us out of the hotels and put us up in Dolo on the mainland. It was only about five miles away but we were sore about it. I had no real hostility towards the officers but at times they put rank first, in other words, I'm alright Jack and you do what you like. I thought, hang on, we have all been in this together. We have all devoted our lives to our country so we should have equal rights to enjoy the fruits of peace regardless of whether you are an officer or a private.

It was whilst they were in Dolo that the Allies formally accepted the official surrender of the German Army in Italy on 2nd May 1945.

Of course we celebrated but, unlike the infantry, we still had work to do. There was still the sick and injured to care for and transfer back from our field ambulance to the base hospitals. Once that was done some of us followed the patients back and were posted to hospital duties. I was lucky because I was selected to accompany an officer on sick parades and we set off in a jeep with our bivouacs to tour the beautiful Italian countryside again. I liked that job and I probably got it because I was a sportsman.

However, the heady atmosphere engendered by peace was fleeting. Four days after VE day the Black Cats had to speed north-east to protect the Italian - Yugoslav border from the threat of invasion by communist Yugoslav partisans.

An advance party from the 214th led the way to the border town of Malfalcone and the whole unit followed the next day. Lectures were quickly held on the necessity of their presence and the importance of establishing cordial relations with the local population and Yugoslav troops. Although now muted, the jubilant mood was uncrushed and the men celebrated VE Day with a church service, football match, race meeting and a special dinner with beer and locally purchased alcohol. On 19th May, the 214th arranged a day out for the orphans with whom they were billeted. It included a trip to the beach, games, a party and music from the pipe band of the London Scottish Regiment.[174]

And there was one famous football match that became the high point of my army sporting career.

It was decided that the British Army in Italy would challenge the local Italian civilian team to a game of football. They picked the team and we had some very good players, people that had turned out for Sheffield Wednesday, Hartlepool, and Birmingham, but one by one the goalkeepers dropped out. In the end they phoned up the unit and said, "You've got a goalkeeper, the name of Earl?" "Yes" "Can he play tomorrow?" "Yes." I must have been the sixth choice. There was quite a big crowd of supporters there and it rained but the funny thing was, when it rained, I always played better. We finally won 2:1 and I saved a penalty.

The unit was thus reverting to its peacetime role but although the men were kept entertained they would not be distracted from the one recurring question.

We'd been away for three or four years so not surprisingly, everyone was asking, when are we going back home?

On 24th May, William's question was unexpectedly answered. Captain Elliott's request that he should be given a compassionate posting to the UK had been granted. William was due to leave for England the next day.

10
Reunited with Mary

I was overjoyed. I couldn't believe that I was finally being allowed to go home. The other men were delighted for me but it was tinged with jealousy because they were just as desperate to get back. I immediately wrote to Mary and told her that I was coming home and not to be surprised if she saw me sometime in June or July.

The next day, I packed up all my kit and said my farewells. While it was sad to leave my friends, I'd had enough of the army. It still felt foreign to me and I didn't look back when I left.

There were quite a few of us leaving from various units and we travelled across to Naples where we boarded a ship for Toulon and then on to England. I was so excited that I couldn't even remember the journey back.

When we docked on 10th June 1945, we were told that we were being posted to the RAMC regimental HQ at Aldershot. I'd never been there before so I thought, oh God, this will be grim because they'll expect us to look absolutely perfect even though we'd been overseas for three years. We smartened ourselves up as much as we could before we arrived but as it was, nothing was said about our well worn uniforms and grimy skin. We were given a billet for the night and told to report to the orderly room next day to find out where we'd be posted. We were warned that it could be anywhere in the British Isles, including the north of Scotland. That was the last thing I wanted to hear. To be in Britain, yet facing the prospect of being hundreds of miles away from Mary was torture and I had to fight the urge to leap on a train and go AWOL.

The next day, I reported to the orderly officer. He asked me, "Are you married? And your wife is at Hammersmith?" "Yes," I said. "Well," he said, "They want one or two medical men at 18 Company, Queen Alexandra's military hospital Millbank, (QAMH Millbank) in London. You'll be there for a minimum of six months. Right, you can go home now and report to Millbank on 14th July." That was it. That was my ticket home.

I grabbed my kit bag, got a travel warrant and caught the first available train to London. As I sat there looking out of the window, I saw some of the damage that had been done to the centre of London. When I got off it felt like the post-war euphoria was lingering because everybody was friendly and happy. Yet, as I got closer to home, doubts began seeping into my mind about going straight to Mary's. I needed to know how the land lay with her and how she was coping before I saw her again, so I decided to go to my Mother's instead.

Mother got quite a shock when I knocked on the door that evening. She was surprised that I looked so different. I was fitter, heavier, sunburnt and had the presence of a man, not the boy that had left in 1942. I dumped my kit bag on the ground and embraced her. She was overcome with emotion and couldn't stop crying. It was wonderful to see her and be back home. Once I'd settled in, I asked about Mary. Mother reassured me that she was coping. After a restless night's sleep in my old bed, I squeezed into my old civilian clothes, got some directions for the Peabody Estate and left to see my family.

I walked to Shepherd's Bush Green. The area had been badly damaged. Some buildings were still in ruins and Mary's old terrace had gone completely. The trams were running freely so I caught one down to Hammersmith Broadway. I found the Gaumont Cinema and just behind were the big blocks of flats on the Peabody Estate.

The Peabody Estate was a six acre site in Hammersmith which had been bought by an American philanthropist to provide decent social housing for the artisans and labouring poor of London. It comprised of 284 flats split into 32 blocks and 34 cottages, pram sheds, a coal store, purpose built laundry

Chapter 10 **Reunited with Mary**

block and a separate bathhouse.[175] It was functional rather than attractive and had been bombed during the war.

I located number 90 and knocked on the door.

Mary wasn't surprised to see me because she had been expecting me for days. When she opened the door we just stood there and looked at each other, delighted and relieved that we had both survived. It wasn't a rapturous welcome but she was still the girl of my dreams, the one I'd yearned to return to. We embraced, but after three years apart, we were like strangers and in the back of my mind I felt so sorry about what she had gone through. I could see its impact on her face and she looked older than I'd expected but just being near her again brought me such joy and happiness. After a bit I said, "I told you I'd come back," and we held each other until this little boy appeared from inside the flat. "Who's this?" I asked, "This is David," she said. He just stood there looking blankly at me. He was now 4-years-old and had no idea who I was.

Mary led me into their little flat and I looked around at the odd sticks of furniture she had scraped together. There were two bedrooms, a sitting room with a stove for cooking and heating, a separate toilet and a little kitchen. The baths were in the communal bathhouse in the square. I don't know why, but I had expected nothing to have changed in my absence. Now it sunk in that my home life had changed beyond recognition. Before I left, Mary and I had always stayed at my Mother's house and when David came along she lived with Cissie and I went to visit them there. Mary and I had never lived alone together and I'd had no real experience of being a husband or a father, yet here I was, married and living with a wife I'd never lived with and a son who didn't know me. I felt totally disorientated. However, I had to set that feeling aside because I needed to get to the bottom of what had happened to Mary.

It was painful for her to explain, so we discussed it very gently and as she told me how it happened I fell in love with her all over again. Mary had tried to deal with it by imagining that she was recovering from an attack of flu or something like that but I felt sad and angry that I had not been there to

Right: Mary Earl when living on the Peabody Estate and awaiting William's return.

protect her. It was clear that when Cissi was told she hadn't given Mary much support and my Mother had jumped to the wrong conclusion so their relationship had become strained. The only thing that I could do now was set the record straight. With Mary's blessing, I went back to my Mother's the next day, told her what had really happened and that I was moving in with Mary right away. Mum confessed that she had suspected that it was not a straightforward matter and now that she knew, she wanted to restore the loving relationship they'd had before.

With all the strings tied up, Mary and I drew a line under the incident and didn't mention it again. Instead, we discussed snippets from the lives we'd lived apart. Mary told me about being evacuated to Leeds, being bombed out and moving to the Peabody Estate. I talked about the places I visited. When I described Italy to Mary she said, "I'd love to go one day." I always used to joke, "Sorry Mary darling, but we'd better let another few years go by. I don't want anybody to call me Daddy." She used to laugh. She knew I wasn't serious. I never mentioned the injuries we saw or the horrifying moments. I kept that to myself.

One thing I became aware of was that I'd still been courting Mary in my letters home. Inexplicably, I kept thinking that I was still courting her now, this time in her own little flat and there was a third person involved, our son.

Chapter 10 Reunited with Mary

I don't think I resented the fact that David was there, but I'd had no practice at being a Dad and it took me about a year to get good at it.

When it came round to reporting to QAMH Millbank on 14th July, all I wanted to do was be with Mary and finally start this married life of ours. Hospital orderlies and ward staff normally lived in Millbank barracks and it felt dreadful having to pack up my kit to leave again. I tried to be cheerful and said, "I'll only be at Millbank and I'll be able to see you from time to time."

I arrived early and reported to the orderly officer. "Have you got any dental knowledge?" he said. "No Sir." I replied. "Oh well, you'll soon pick it up. The dental officer's orderly has been demobbed and we want you to take his place. You'll be assisting Captain Bingham," he said. I knew the name because Morris Bingham was a famous cross-country runner. When I reported to him I was struck by his relaxed manner. Captain Bingham was so unlike what I was used to. He said, "Ah yes. How are you? You're under my command now and these are your duties. You are to report here at 9 o'clock each morning and at 4 o'clock you shall take the impressions of all the dentures to Knightsbridge and pick them up and bring them back the next morning. You won't have to go on parades or anything like that but you will have to wear your army dress." "Oh," I said, "Do I live in here?" "No," he replied, " You'll live at home so you can take all your kit back and you'll only work a nine to four job provided you bring the dentures back in the morning." I was so excited that I could hardly wait to get home. At the end of the day, I rushed back to Mary and said, "It's wonderful. I can live at home." I think I was more excited about that than coming back from Italy. I could not believe that I was back doing a normal job again.

We only worked during the weekdays and all sorts of people came to see Captain Bingham. I used to meet them and take their particulars. I helped with the extractions and when Captain Bingham found out about my pharmacy experience, he said, "Ah, you'll know how to mix the compounds for fillings. You just need so much of this and so much of that and just mix it up." It was almost exactly like being back at Boots. Sometimes after work

Mary, David and I would go out for a walk and once in a while David stayed with my Mum so that Mary and I could go to the pictures.

I was often asked what I had done in the war and when I said that I was in the medical corps, some would say, "Ah, what an easy job. You just had to wait until the battle was over and go and pick up the injured and bring them back. That's easy." That didn't worry me too much because those that we'd helped knew what we'd done. When Mary heard, she said that people had said the same thing to her when I was abroad. She said she used to feel very indignant and would quietly set them right. Some people thought that I was in the RAMC because I was a conscientious objector so then it was my turn to set them right. A few ex-soldiers used to joke and say, "RAMC, that's short for Rob All My Comrades." I'd heard that one before and, yes, there were one or two in our company that probably would have stooped to it if they'd had the chance, but I never met a Red Cross man who said, "Look, this is what I took from a dead German or a dead Englishman." A favourite question was, 'Who did you save when you only had one stretcher, a German soldier or an English soldier?' I told them that we didn't discriminate. We had to decide who had the most serious injury, but in reality, when you were out there, you always had in the back of your mind that the Allies came first. Those that we had helped asked me where we had got the courage to do it. I told them we weren't courageous. We were trained to do what we did and we followed our training. I didn't tell them that I thought it was ridiculous that we tried to repair them or save their lives only for them to be sent back to the front line to be killed or injured again.

It was great working there but I could tell from the Londoners I met that they had changed. Not at first, because everyone was still happy and having a wonderful time, but after a few months it became noticeable that people were not as easy going as they had been before the war. They were still friendly but you could tell that the stress and strain had left its mark and the lovely openness and generosity of the pre-war years had gone. People had become more interested in going their own way rather than thinking of how they could help and care for their neighbours.

Chapter 10 Reunited with Mary

I was at Millbank until I was due to be demobbed in March 1946. All was going well until the 1st March when I came home from work and didn't feel good at all. I got worse during the night so Mary left me in bed, got her coat and went straight to a public call box. She phoned QAMH Millbank and an ambulance was sent immediately. By the time it arrived, I was in a great deal of pain and couldn't move a muscle. I was diagnosed with rheumatic fever and admitted to Millbank hospital. I was treated with a mixture of sodium salicylate every two hours and it tasted horrible. I spent three weeks there before they transferred me to Queen Alexandra's military hospital Horley, (QAMH Horley) on 17th April.

When I'd more or less recovered I had a final check-up. Unfortunately they discovered little growths in the marrow of my bones so I had to stay on until they operated on my upper forearm to take them out. Luckily, they were non-malignant so I was discharged. I returned to QAMH Millbank but because I'd been absent for so long someone else had taken my job. It was such a shame because I'd loved every moment of it and I was concerned that I would be posted somewhere away from London. I was relieved when I learnt that I was going to assist at the pension panels in Westminster and could continue to live at home.

The panels were made up of two to three doctors who calculated what sort of pension an ill or injured soldier should receive. The worse his injuries, the more he got. They ran from 9.30am to 4.30pm and there were three nursing orderlies to see to the soldiers' needs. We'd take their details when they arrived, get them something to eat or drink and help them into the panel. We had a few amputees but most of the chaps had mental injuries and they were in a shocking state. They had been totally traumatised by the war. They were very, very quiet, almost as if they weren't fully conscious of life going on around them, in fact, they reminded me of men coming round from an anaesthetic. I hadn't had much experience of this because those with mental injuries were generally evacuated out of the field ambulance and taken straight back to the base hospital or England.

I had great sympathy for them and would think how easily it could have been me standing there. Imagine, you could have two friends standing next to each other chatting and suddenly BANG! one of them has his head blown off and the other is left standing there looking at his friend's body. That sort of thing affected you and it could happen over and over again like it did at Anzio. Frank's capture affected me but at least I knew he was alive and I was sent back to recover in Sorrento. I was lucky, some infantrymen had to stay on the front line until they went mad.

There wasn't much work to do at the panels so we'd do crosswords or eat cake a lot of the time. I was there for two months then it was time for me to be demobbed again. Hence on the 4th July, I packed all my kit and left home in my uniform for the last time. I stayed the night at Millbank barracks ready to leave first thing in the morning with the other men due to be demobbed next day.

Early on 5th July 1946, I jumped into an army truck for the last time. Upon arrival at the demob centre in Horley we signed lots of papers, I handed in my uniform and was given a grey spun demob suit. I received four weeks' pay plus any bonuses that I'd got, like all my Italian pay which I'd saved because I'd lived off the illicit proceeds of selling army blankets. I got my travel warrant and caught the train back to London where I blended in with thousands of other men sporting their demob suits. After six years of military service I could finally start to live the life I'd always wanted to live.

By now, I had got used to being a husband and father but Mary and I had never had a proper honeymoon, so after I was discharged we spoke to the two Mothers about going away on our own. Cissie, as always, was not too happy about it but my Mother was emphatic. She said, "I'll look after little David, you two go away and get to know each other again."

Hastings was our special place so we decided to go back there. We went up to White Rock Gardens and watched people play tennis and Mary would say, "Do you remember when I got up here and I had to tell you I couldn't play ?" We'd wander hand-in-hand over the cliffs to a place called Lover's Seat. We talked and talked just like we did before the war. It was wonderful

Chapter 10 **Reunited with Mary**

Above: Far left William sitting next to Frank at the inaugural reunion of the 214th in 1947.

and after those three weeks we felt that, at long last, we were a couple again. We returned home at the start of the fourth week because the money was about to run out and I had to return to work. We were also eager to see David again and when we collected him from my Mum's it felt like we were starting afresh.

I was on the army reserve list until 1959 in case hostilities broke out with the Soviet Union, but I had remained on Boots' books so I got in touch with them. I told them that I was ready to resume work if they still wanted me.

They said, "Yes. We'll arrange for you to come up to Nottingham for three days to see if you are suitable to be a dispensing chemist. We're very short of them because of the war." The comment saddened me because I'd known some of the chemists that had been killed.

The role of a dispensing chemist was very different to that of a chemist's assistant so they had to give me a number of tests including maths. That took me back to my days in Sudbury when I was going to be an accountant. I was good at maths then and I still was so I passed quite well. They posted me to the Ealing Broadway branch to be apprenticed to the dispensing chemist and I spent the next two years on further training and studying for our internal examinations.

It was very, very difficult to adjust to civilian life and that was a problem for thousands of us. Although we had been away for three years, some for four years, we came back expecting to pick up where we had left off, then we saw how the war had affected everyone and everything had changed.

A lot of men were very excited about returning to their wives and girlfriends. When they actually got back and the excitement had worn off, they found that the person to whom they'd returned was different to the person they'd left. Countless relationships broke down for that reason or because they suddenly realised that they had got engaged or married because the war was on, not because they wanted to spend the rest of their lives together. Remember too that thousands of Americans had come over to Britain and some had had affairs with English girls. At one of our annual reunions, one or two of our comrades said, "Oh, I got a divorce when I got back. My wife had already had two children by an American and I wasn't going to stand for that." I thought that was unfair because sex was a natural instinct for men and women and it didn't take note of whether you were married or not. It was also double standards because I knew of only one person who had been absolutely faithful during the war and that was Frank.

Frank wrote to tell me that he was back in England but the first time I saw him was at the inaugural reunion of the 214th in 1947. He was still a gentle bear of a man but he was much more subdued. He didn't want to talk about

Chapter 10 **Reunited with Mary**

the PoW camp and he had the air of a man who had gone through a very bad experience. He'd also not recovered from the injuries he'd sustained during the night mission. His right leg was damaged and his right arm was virtually useless. It was sad to see. He had been a great sportsman and his injuries had taken that away from him.

None of us appreciated how much we'd been affected by the war; the conditions we experienced, the jobs that we'd done and the things we'd survived. Also, the longer we'd been in the army, the greater the chance that the best and the worst of us had been exposed. War allowed us to act heroically. It also allowed us to let off steam in a way that we wouldn't in peacetime, to live out any sexual or violent fantasies and to give free rein to our bad side. This was possible because war provided a cast iron excuse for all bad behaviour.

My Mother would not have recognised the way I had behaved at times. I wish I hadn't stood back when they took the pig or that I'd stolen army blankets so when I returned I treated the period August 1942 to July 1945 as a chunk out of mine, and Mary's, life. We both agreed whatever happened or didn't happen in those three years should be forgotten.

After a time, I realised that I had changed for the better too. I had seen how short and precious life was so I wanted people to be able to live as they wished. I began to listen to people with more interest. I was kinder and showed more respect to my fellow men. Sometimes, I'd pass a man in his demob suit and wonder, did I help you in the war? and I used to get a lovely sense of satisfaction knowing that maybe I'd saved one or two men. You see, although we didn't fight in the infantry sense of the word, we still fought. We fought to save life and our victory was their survival. We had quite a few victories, not bad for a bunch of D-Day Dodgers.

William served in the Royal Army Medical Corps of the British Army for six years and three days. When he was discharged it was noted on his army record that he had been, 'a very willing and hard-working soldier.'[176]

Field Marshall Bernard Law Montgomery said that, 'the contribution made by the RAMC to the Allied victory has been beyond all calculation.' [177]

Epilogue

William lost touch with all his former comrades, apart from Frank who, together with his beloved Marjorie, spent two holidays with William and Mary contentedly watching the boats sailing in and out of Shoreham harbour. The Allens died childless in the 1960s.

William returned to Italy and revisited Salerno, Caserta, Monte Cassino, Sorrento and Rome. He had no desire to return to Anzio.

William qualified as a dispensing chemist in 1948 and remained with Boots the Chemist until 1981. In 1998, William attended the Queen's garden party to celebrate 50 years of the NHS. He was thrilled to be personally thanked by the Queen 'for his service to her people.' Since 1998, William has been involved in charitable work and is currently the vice-president of the Mario Lanza Foundation Trust which helps fund aspiring singers.

In 1952, William and Mary had another child, Michael, to complete their family. They continued to live on the Peabody Estate until 1956 and remained besotted with each other until Mary's death in 1986. After her death, William discovered that Mary had kept all his letters and poems. What happened to Mary in the autumn of 1944 has been kept vague deliberately. Although he knows the full story, William promised Mary that he would never reveal it.

Mary died from the same heart defect that had prevented her from playing tennis with William in 1939. Tragically, she passed it onto David and Michael and they died prematurely, both within seven years of their Mother's death. William was heartbroken. However, in 1991, William met his second wife, Judith Deak, a Hungarian lady, at a Mario Lanza society meeting. They

Epilogue

Above: William aged 101 at home with his medals in 2016.

married in 1992, and spent the next three years touring the world as part of Jose Carreras' production team for his tribute to Mario Lanza.

William's Mother, Bessie, never remarried and followed William and Mary to Sussex when they moved to Shoreham-by-Sea. Bessie continued to play a major role in their lives until her death at the age of 82. William's Father, Ernest, remarried and William was very excited to be reunited with him in the 1950s. William's mother-in-law, Cissie, never took to William but she was very fond of David and Michael.

On 12th May 2016, William celebrated his 101st birthday. He has one daughter-in-law, one step-daughter, three grandchildren, three step-grandchildren, nine great grandchildren and two great, great, grandchildren.

Glossary

167th	167th Field Ambulance RAMC
214th	214th Field Ambulance RAMC
ADS	Advanced Dressing Station
BEF	British Expeditionary Force
Black Cats	56th (London) Division
Capt.	Captain
CCP	Casualty Collecting Post
CCS	Casualty Clearing Station
C.O	Commanding Officer
DRS	Divisional Rest Station
Grenadier Guards	6th Grenadier Guards
Lt.Col.	Lieutenant Colonel
Maj.	Major
MDS	Main Dressing Station
MEF	Mediterranean Expeditionary Force
M.O	Medical Officer
Oxf/Ox/Oxen and Bucks	7th Oxfordshire and Buckinghamshire Light Infantry
Pte.	Private
Queen's	2nd/5th Queen's Royal Regiment (West Surrey)
	2nd/6th Queen's Royal Regiment (West Surrey)
	2nd/7th Queen's Royal Regiment (West Surrey)
RAP	Regimental Aid Post
RASC	Royal Army Service Corps
RAMC	Royal Army Medical Corps
R.F	Royal Fusiliers (City of London Regiment)
R.M.O	Regimental Medical Officer
RSB	Regimental Stretcher Bearer
Scots Guards	1st Battalion Scots Guards
Sgt.	Sergeant
WWCP	Walking Wounded Collecting Post

Acknowledgements

Firstly, I would like to thank Ian Bayley of Sabrestorm Publishing who took a great leap of faith when he accepted an unfinished book by a new author and who has waited so patiently for the final manuscript. Ian's patience, passion and support for Blood and Bandages has been invaluable.

Thanks to Karl French of the Literary Consultancy who provided insightful and practical advice on how I could fulfil this story's potential.

Mr Rob McIntosh from the Army Medical Services museum has continuously gone the extra mile whenever I have needed his help and my thanks go to him and the AMS museum for allowing me to use their photographs.

This book could not have been written without the records at the National Archives and the help of their efficient staff so I extend my thanks to them.

I owe a huge debt of gratitude to the exceptional writers whose work I have I relied upon to research this project. They include James Holland, Lloyd Clark, Eric Linklater, Douglas Orgill, Normal Lewis, Matthew Parker, the unknown author of Operation Achse, Anthony Cotterell, Redmond McLaughlin and Antony Beevor. It has been a pleasure to research this project because of the elegance of their prose and the depth of their knowledge.

This project has taken many years to come to fruition and throughout that time my family and friends have been tremendously supportive and encouraging. They have not begrudged me cancelling things at the last minute, talking endlessly about the book and moaning about the length of time it was taking to complete. Thank you all.

I would also like to thank the following individually; Dave Dennison for his steadying influence when things got rocky, my dear friend and actor, Sandra Clark, for commenting on endless drafts and having a clarity of vision throughout and to my writing partner, Leia Vogelle, whose forensic analysis of the final draft was invaluable.

Finally my thanks go to my marvellous husband Richard, who has selflessly encouraged my dream of being a writer and our wonderful son Tom, who has been shunted from one babysitter to the next and who has been left to fend for himself while I finished this book. Without you both, this book would have remained but a dream.

Footnotes

Introduction

1. 'to effect the rapid evacuation… and wounded' *RAMC Training Manual* 1935 HMSO p.101 paragraph 277
2. 'the simplest accommodation and treatment' ibid p.82 paragraph 179
3. It contained 238 men…Chaplain's batman Nicholls, T.B *Organisation, Strategy, Tactics of the Army Medical Services in War.* Bailliere Tindall and Cox 1937 p.103
4. Around 40 wounded ibid p.72
5. 'established as far forward…will permit' ibid p.77
6. about 2,000 yards behind ibid p.78
7. The advanced dressing station could… control a haemorrhage' ibid p.79
8. two to five miles ibid p.89
9. 'two to four ambulances' ibid p.106
10. 400-500 cases ibid p.89

Chapter One – The Early Years

11. over one million French…were missing Westwell, Ian *World War 1 Day by Day* Spellmount Limited, Kent 2005 p.46
12. 4000 poison gas cylinders ibid p. 60
13. at 4.48 on 1st September Beevor, Antony *The Second World War* Weidenfeld & Nicolson 2012 p. 27
14. at 8.00pm Poland requested…Britain and France' Retrieved from: http://history.co.uk/study-topics/history-of-ww2/poland

Chapter Two – William and Mary

15. 'This morning the British Ambassador… war with Germany' Retrieved from: www.bbc.co/uk/archive
16. 'News of the double declaration of war… joy in Warsaw' Beevor, Op.cit p.35
17. Over the next five weeks… troops followed. ibid p.39
18. By September 1940…army corps. Crew, FAE, *History of World War Two, The Army Medical Services, Administrative Volume* HMSO 1953 p.309
19. The Royal Army Medical Corps… by September 1940 ibid p.309
20. It was to… initially assigned. The National Archives (TNA) WO 177/756
21. 'The French and British… shamefully' Beevor Op.cit p.39
22. 'lives unworthy of life' Beevor Op.cit p.57
23. 'peaceful occupation' Beevor Op.cit p.90
24. 'We have been defeated.' Beevor Op.cit p.114
25. 45,000 men Beevor Op.cit p.131
26. Over the next nine days… vessels Beevor Op.cit p.139
27. The 167th … at Margate, Ramsgate and Broadstairs TNA WO 177/756
28. 'What General Weygand…their finest hour.' Retrieved from: www.bbc.co.uk/schoolradio/subjects/history/ww2clips/speeches/churchill_finest_hour
29. They arrived at…5pm. TNA WO 177/818
30. 'Intake contains…of men' ibid
31. 'eliminate the English Motherland…full extent' RAFairman. (July 16 2010 6.28pm) *Directive 16 Eliminate the English Motherland.* Retrieved from: http://rafairman.wordpress.com/category/battle-of-britain-70th-anniversary
32. After six weeks… A and B. TNA Wo 177/818
33. 'a vast armada two miles wide' Putland L Alan. Battle of Britain Historical Society (13 August 2010 11.20) *Sunday September 15th 1940 details of the mornings action* Retrieved from: www.battleofbritain1940.net/0041.html
34. 'in total a combined force…30 miles' Battle of Britain Historical Society (12 August 2010

Footnotes

	15.31) Sunday September 15th 1940 (afternoon) Retrieved from: www.battleofbritain1940.net/0041.html
35	Meanwhile…variety of subjects TNA WO 177/818
36	Lt-Col Marshall's… without permission TNA WO 177/818
37	On 5th September… Coles Dane House. ibid
38	The Nazi ideology…anti-semitic Beevor Op.cit p.228
39	On 14th January…exams TNA WO 177/818
40	Consequently on 16th…Home in Ipswich ibid
41	By now…overseas ibid
42	The 214th…cancelled ibid

Chapter Three – William and Frank

43	'the largest, longest… War Two' Dempsey Janet. (Thu.10 Sep 2009 11.00GMT) *The battle that frightened Churchill: the war in the Atlantic* at 1.52 Podcast retrieved from: http://www.nationalarchives/gov.uk/podcasts/38308-play.htm
44	fed, fuelled and fighting ibid at 6.32
45	'much enjoyed… ranks' TNA WO 177/819
46	Meantime… Cape Town ibid
47	On 23rd October … Cape Town TNA WO 177/756
48	Hence, HMT Lancashire…Tunisia TNA WO 177/819
49	The 167th proceeded to …camp TNA WO 177/756
50	while the 214th … Kirkuk TNA WO 177/819
51	By 22nd December… 37 Indian Field Ambulance ibid
52	'an attacker should…muster' Parker, Matthew, Monte Cassino *The Story of the Hardest-fought Battle of World War Two,* Headline 2003 p.3
53	Indeed… left Baghdad TNA WO 177/819
54	The next day …front line ibid
55	'the Boches were…Enfidaville' Delaforce, Patrick, *Churchill's Desert Rats in North Africa, Burma, Sicily and Italy* Sutton Publishing Limited 2002 p.140 quoting the words of Sergeant Wardrop, 5 RTR
56	Consequently three of A company… Enfidaville TNA WO 177/819

Chapter Four – Enfidaville

57	In light of …further back ibid
58	'Medical Officers and men…replace' TB Nicholls etc Op.cit ibid p.77
59	On 26th April 1943… Enfidaville TNA WO 177/819
60	The collecting…Queens TNA WO 177/756
61	On 9th May…driver ibid.
62	'During the search…sniping TNA WO 177/819
63	'Mediterranean adventure' Parker, Op.cit p.4
64	'to eliminate Italy…troops' Linklater, Eric *The Campaign in Italy* HMSO 1951 p.48
65	Italy had 34 divisions Operation Achse, (5 July 2016 12.49) Retrieved from: https://en.wikipedia.org/wiki/Operation_Achse
66	'learned how to…Africa' Parker, Op.cit p.7 citing General Bradley, American II Corps
67	130,000 German… had been captured. Ibid p.8
68	Mountain warfare…immediately TNA WO 177/819
69	Unaware of…north of Rome. Operation Asche Op.cit
70	'a shrunken man…psychologically.' Beevor, Op.cit p.599
71	Consequently…activated Operation Asche Op.cit
72	In negotiations…reprisals ibid.
73	'It was the …Mediterranean' ibid.
74	Germans took 650,000..slave labour Beevor, Op.cit p.606
75	94,000 mainly fascists Operation Asche Op.cit
76	'the Italian armed.. exist' ibid.

Chapter Five – The invasion of Italy

77	Meantime, on the adjoining…dig slit trenches TNA WO 177/756
78	By first light… main dressing station TNA WO 177/819
79	By the …hospital ship TNA WO 204/8264
80	gunshot wound to the buttock TNA WO 177/819
81	'It was now apparent…opposed' TNA WO 204/8264
82	One of them…leg TNA WO 177/819
83	'Proceed direct…bridges' TNA WO 177/756
84	At 8.30am the next day… an ADS ibid
85	'10th September…did not know' ibid
86	That night the 9th … Grenadier Guards. TNA WO 204/8264
87	'Unable to cope…casualties' TNA 177/756
88	'very excitable state' ibid
89	In fact they were retreating…at gunpoint TNA 204/8264
90	A few hours later…excitable state TNA 177/756
91	'Tend to infect other people' Cotterell, Anthony *RAMC – an authoritative account prepared with the assistance of the Army Medical Department of the War Office and the R.A.M.C.* Hutchinson & Co London 1942-3 p. 95
92	'and the division…beaches' TNA WO 204/8264
93	The naval smoke screen…winched off' ibid
94	'In the first…caps' ibid
95	'The situation is extremely critical' Clark, Lloyd *Anzio The Friction of War* Headline Publishing Group 2006 p. 23
96	Battapaglia…bodies of their men. TNA WO 177/756
97	the 214th's…wounded TNA WO 177/819
98	Overall the Americans… 5,500 Beevor, Op.cit p.609
99	'Italy is a boot…top' Parker, Op.cit p.xvi
100	In Sicily…mountains ibid p.13
101	The Black Cats… Prisoners of War TNA 177/819
102	250 divisional battle casualties…by the sick ibid
103	Lieutenant Colonel Richards…100 per cent TNA WO 226/606
104	'varied in width…of its length' TNA WO 204/8264
105	'it was the most…at the rear' ibid
106	scheduled to start at 8.50pm on 12th October. ibid
107	'In spite of…stop the operation' ibid
108	It was granted…wounded ibid
109	By 31st October… 800 men Linklater, Op.cit p.134
110	'Our troops were…prehistoric times' Parker, Op.cit p.41 quoting Ernie Pyle.

Chapter Six – Frank's capture

111	'it was as bare…foot down' Wheatley C M Monte Camino – The First Battle, November 1943 Papers May 1945 (10 July 2016 12.16) Retrieved from: www.italystarassociation.org.uk
112	'Platoon Commanders…imminent' ibid
113	'All went well…was to follow' ibid
114	'of an intensity … First World War' Parker, Op.cit p.64 quoting Lieutenant-General Fridolin von Senger und Etterlin
115	Indeed…badly shaken TNA WO 177/756
116	By 7th Dec… died from this wounds ibid
117	Instead Frank was…camp in Bavaria TNA WO 392/1
118	'big and costly attack' TNA 204/8269
119	'two weeks of… rest and recreation' ibid

Footnotes

Chapter Seven – Anzio

120 the German garrison…3,000 vehicles Clark, Op.cit p.115
121 76,400 Allied troops…100,000 German troops ibid p.158
122 'the largest self-supporting… the world' (8 Aug 2016 19.40) Retrieved from: www.pbs.org/thewar/at_home_communication_propaganda.htm
123 'The British and…rushed to Anzio' TNA WO 204/8269
124 Within 24 hours…been lost. ibid
125 The situation…be given away ibid
126 'Each was some…bottom of these gullies' ibid
127 'It passed right…more uncertain' TNA WO 204/8269
128 Two men in … order to return. TNA WO 177/819
129 'the total area…decidedly unhealthy spot' TNA WO 204/8269
130 'By 25th January… defiant one' ibid
131 'contact with the…critical and unpleasant' ibid
132 Staff Sergeant Ross…with a blowtorch Clark, Op.cit p.322
133 After a short return…day off duty. TNA WO 177/819
134 Despite their … minor sicknesses ibid
135 'It remained…and training' TNA 204/8269

Chapter Eight – The price of friendship

136 The accommodation…watched a concert. TNA WO 177/819
137 The 214th docked…leave in Cairo ibid
138 On 25th April… Pyramid of Cheops ibid
139 'At the…a liberated ally' TNA 204/8264
140 'Had we in Italy…re-training periods' ibid
141 'We have not…a dominating height' ibid
142 'The platoon is…and causes casualties' ibid
143 At 4.55am… established in France Clark, Lloyd Operation Overlord: D-Day to Paris 17 Feb 2011 Retrieved from: www.bbc.co.history/history/worldwars/wwtwo/overlord_d_day_paris_01.shtml
144 'largest and most…war so far' Soviet Storm: World War II — In The East. Episode . 11. Operation Bagration. 31 Oct 2013 StarMedia at 8.06 Retrieved from: https://www.youtube.com/watch?v=i6UkVl3ZFuI
145 2.4 milion…5,300 aircraft ibid at 12.18
146 By 10th July…day passes to Rome TNA WO 177/819
147 'it is reported …the Italian women' Lewis, Norman, *Naples '44 An Intelligence Officer in the Italian Labyrinth* Eland London 2002 p.129
148 While General Commander-in-Chief…the abuses TNA WO 204/9765
149 When they arrived…then beheaded Lewis, Op.cit p.134

Chapter Nine – D-Day Dodgers

150 On its way…forthcoming operation. TNA WO 177/819
151 'Non-stop to the Po.' Orgill, Douglas, *The Gothic Line* Heinmann London 1967 p.38
152 were forbidden to leave… completed by dawn. TNA WO 177/819
153 'when we looked down…appeared suicidal' Orgill Op.cit p.46
154 A Company was put on…leading battalion TNA WO 177/819
155 'a plentiful supply…of the Apennines' TNA WO 204/8265
156 Two days later…wounded 200. TNA WO 177/819
157 'From these heights… infantry to attack' Orgill, Op cit.107
158 These two…with very severe wounds TNA WO 177/819
159 'battle of the Salerno…Monte Camino' TNA WO 204/8269
160 Fourteen thousand…the Gothic Line Orgill, Op cit p.194
161 on 11th October…200 bed CRS. TNA WO 177/819
162 'Throughout the army…Battle of the Rivers' Linklater Op. cit p.370

155

163 'Water was now…than high ground.' Orgill Op.cit p.161
164 'After all the effort…kept the date.' ibid p.214
165 Ballad of the D-Day Dodgers. Compiled and edited by Major Hamish Henderson. Retrieved from: http://lyricsplayground.com/alpha/songs/d/ddaydodgers.shtml contributed by Mel June 2004
166 D-Day was set…the Fantail TNA WO 177/819
167 Four were needed…their return flight ibid
168 In previous… prone to minefield. TNA WO 204/8264
169 'the battle is moving forward very quickly' TNA WO 177/819
170 'had taken on the appearance of a rout' ibid
171 'a scene of…the German Army' Linklater Op.cit p.464
172 A Company was…DUKWS and Fantails TNA WO 177/819
173 The infantry commenced…just after midnight ibid
174 On 19th May…London Scottish Regiment ibid

Chapter Ten – Reunited with Mary

175 The Peabody estate…bathhouse Retrieved from: http://www.peabody.org.uk/about-us/our-history/history-of-our-estates#hammersmith
176 'A very willing…soldier' Notification of impending release of William Earl dated 5th July 1946
177 'the contribution made…beyond all calculation' McLaughlin, Redmond *The Royal Army Medical Corps* Leo Cooper Ltd London 1972 p. 104

Bibliography

Beevor, Antony   *The Second World War* Weidenfeld & Nicolson 2014
Clark, Lloyd   *Anzio The Friction of War* Headline 2007
Cotterall, Anthony   *RAMC An authoritative account prepared with the assistance of the Army Medical Department of the War Office and R.A.M.C* Hutchinson 1943/4
Hastings, Max   *Finest Years Churchill as Warlord 1940-45* HarperPress 2009
Delaforce, Patrick   *Churchill's Desert Rats in North Africa, Burma, Sicily and Italy* Pen and Sword Military 2009
Holland, James   *Italy's Sorrow A year of War 1944-45* HarperPress 2009
Lewis, Norman   *Naples '44 An intelligence Officer in the Italian Labyrinth* Eland 2002
Linklater, Eric   *The Campaign in Italy* HMSO 1951
McLaughlin, Redmond *The Royal Army Medical Corps* Leo Cooper Ltd 1972
Orgill, Douglas   *The Gothic Line (The Autumn Campaign in Italy 1944)* Heineman 1967
Parker, Matthew   *Monte Cassino The Story of the Hardest-fought Battle of World War Two* Headline 2003
The National Archives   *WO 177/756, WO 177/757, WO 177/818, WO 177/819, WO 204/ 8264, WO 204/8265, WO 204/8267,WO 204/ 8269, WO 204/8181, WO 204/9765, WO 222/606, WO 222/426, WO 392/1*

Film and Podcasts

Simply Home Entertainment   *British Campaigns Italy 1943 -1945*   2010
Dempsey, Janet   *The Battle that frightened Churchill: the war in the Atlantic* National Archives Podcast

Electronic Sources

en.wikipedia.org   Operation Achse
www.italystarassociation.org.uk   Wheatley CM   *Account of first battle of Monte Camino*
www.youtube.com   *Soviet Storm: World War I1 In The East. Episode. 11. Operation Bagration*
www.bbc.co.history   Clark, Lloyd *Operation Overlord*
          Cruickshank, Dan *The German Threat to Britain in World War Two*
www.battleofbritain1940.net. Putland, Alan Battle of Britain Historical Society. *The Battle of Britain 1940*
rafairman.wordpress.com   Directive 16 Eliminate the English Motherland

Index

56th (London) Division *(see Black Cats)*
167th Field Ambulance 22, 26-7, 30, 31, 47, 49, 51, 62-3, 74, 75-9, 94, 112
214th Field Ambulance 22, 27-36, 40, 44-57, 62-5, 75, 83, 87, 89-90, 107, 111-2, 115, 118, 122-3, 126, 132-3, 135-6

A
Abley MM, Sgt B M, 33, 63-4, 73-74
Allen, Pte Frank 29-30, 40, 42, 44-5, 55-60, 61-2, 66-7, 68, 73-5, 82, 84, 88, 90-1, 95-6, 109-10, 112-3, 144-5, 146-7
America, 35, 39, 43, 47, 50-1, 64
Anzio, 97, 99-107, 109-10, 114, 115, 133, 144
Astor MP, Viscountess Nancy, 128, 131
Atlantic, *battle of*, 43-5, *engima naval codes*, 43-4, *wolfpacks*, 43-5
Axis forces, 33, 40, 47, 50, 55-6, 62

B
Badoglio, Marshal Pietro, 70-1
Black Cats, 27-8, 36, 41, 49, 51-2, 62, 64, 69, 79, 83, 86, 89, 94, 97, 100, 106, 115, 119, 121, 123, 126, 132-135,

167th Infantry Brigade, 28, 69, 75, 87, 94, 105, 126
168th Infantry Brigade, 28, 69, 105, 113
169th Infantry Brigade, 28, 56, 69, 84, 86-7, 89-90, 94, 100, 105, 113-4,
8th Royal Fusiliers, 75-8,
9th Royal Fusiliers, 75-6, 87
Grenadier Guards, 28, 76, 89-90, 201
Guards, 84, 87,
intelligence, 113,
Oxen & Bucks, 63-4, 87,
Queen's, 28-9, 30, 49, 52, 55-6, 62, 73-5, 87, 95, 100, 112, 122-3, 132-5
recruitment, 113,
regimental stretcher bearers, 8, 56-7, 58, 63-4
Scots Guards, 90,
training, 113
Boots the Chemist, 12-14, 25, 145-6
Britain, 11, 22-3, 26, 48-9,
appeasement, 18,
battle of, 28-9, 32
Blitz, 32, 34
King George VI, 67,

157

Phoney War, 23,
rationing, 34, 36, 38
British Expeditionary Force, 22,
Dunkirk, 25-6, 105

C
Cape Town 45-6
Casablanca Conference 50, 64, 69
Catchpole, Pte George 30, 82, 112-3, 116-8
Churchill, Winston 25, 27, 35, 40, 45, 50, 64, 68
Clark, Gen Mark 69, 79-80, 99, 114, 119
Cork, Cyril 16, 18, 38

D
D-Day Dodgers, 128, 147,
ballad of 130-1

E
Earl, Bessie 11-23, 25-7, 34, 36, 38-9, 40, 90, 119, 123, 138-40, 144, 147
Earl, David 40-1, 108-11, 139, 140-2, 144, 145
Earl, Ernest 11-4, 16-7, 19-21, 25-6, 34
Earl, Mary *(see Standen, Mary)*
Egypt, 27, 33, 40, 51, 109, 111-13, 114-5,
Cairo, 111-13
Eighth Army, 51, 52, 62, 69, 71, 79-80, 119, 121, 126, 128-9
Elliott, Capt J.M 118, 128, 136
Enfidaville, *(also see night missions)* 52, 55-65, 73
Bou-Fiche Road, 63-4
joint dressing station 66-7, 68

F
Field Ambulance, *(also see 214th 169th)*, 7, 59-61,
advanced dressing station, 8-9, 30, 54, 59, 60-1, 62, 69, 74-5, 94, 95, 102, 105, 122, 124-5, 132
casualty collecting post, 52, 56-7, 59, 60-1, 62, 100, 102, 104-5,
main dressing station, 9, 30, 36, 49, 54, 61, 62, 78-9, 83, 90, 92, 94, 95, 105, 107, 109, 125
regimental aid post 8-9, 56, 63, 74-5, 76, 122
walking wounded collecting post, 9, 66
Fifth Army, 69, 71, 80, 83, 87, 88, 119, 121, 126-7
First World War, 11, 18, 82, 94
France, 11, 22, 25, 26, 99
appeasement, 18,
Poland, 18-9,
surrender of, 27-8, 42
invasion of, 114,
battle of Normandy 114, 127

G
Germany, 11, 18-9, 21-3, 25, 28, 32, 33, 39, 40, 43, 45, 64, 69-71
Gothic Line, 81, 114, 119, 121-26,
A and B tents, 123-4,
River Foglia, 122,
Gemmano ridge, 122-3
Minefields, 132-3
Mondaino, 122
Goums, 114, 118
Gustav Line, 88, 91, 99, 114
Mignano Gap, 89,
Mte Camino 1st battle, 89-90,
Mte Camino 2nd battle 94, 123
River Garigliano, 88, 97

H
Harling, Maj *(also see Operation Avalanche)*, 76-8

Index

Hastings, 16-9, 26, 144-5,
Hitler, Adolf, 18-9, 28, 33, 34, 35, 69-71

I
India, 46, 47, 50
Italy, 26-7, 33, 39, 40, 69-71, 114, 140
  Caserta, 83, 84
  Naples, 71, 80, 82, 83-4, 90, 92, 97, 107, 137
  Rome, 71, 88-9, 104, 114, 115-8
  Sorrento, 96, 144
Italian, *autumn,* 126
  landscape, 80-1, 86, 100-2
  prostitution, 82, 116-8
  refugees, 82-3,
  *response to Goums,*118
  surrender of armed forces, 71
  winter 88
Iraq, 47-51

J
Japan, 33, 39, 46, 70
Johnston, Maj *(also see Operation Avalanche),* 76-8, 80

M
Marshall, Lt Col L.P *(also see 214th Field Ambulance),* 28-9, 32-3, 35, 36
Molotov-Ribbentrop Pack, 18-19, 23
Mussolini, Benito, 69-70
Mustoe, Pte H, 63-4

N
Night missions, 62-3
  Bou-Fiche Road, 62-4
  Cascano, 95
North African Campaign, 33, 40, 47, 50-1, 68, 82
Nursing Orderlies, *(also see Royal Army Medical Corps),* 8-9,
  training of, 29-34, 47, 56, 69,
  exams, 34-5, 40,
  in action, 55-61, 73-9, 90, 100-7, 122-5, 141-2

O
Operation Asche, 70-1
Operation Avalanche, 69, 73-80,
  Battapaglia, 75-80,
  Salerno, 69, 71, 73-80, 84, 123
Operation Barbarossa, 35
Operation Bagration, 114, 128
Operation Dragoon, 114, 127
Operation Dynamo, 25
Operation Husky *(see Sicily)*
Operation Overlord, 64, 114
Operation Sealion, 28, 32
Operation Shingle *(see Anzio)*
Operation Torch, 47, 68

P
Peabody Estate Hammersmith, 97, 110, 138-9, 140
Pension Panels, 143-4
Po, 82, 121,
  crossing of, 133-4
Poland, 18-19, 21, 23,

R
Romagna, 121, 124, 126,
  battle for, 126, 132-4
Royal Army Medical Corps, 7, 22, 65, 69, 98, 137, 147
  contentious objectors, 51,
  convalescent hospital, 96
  Geneva Convention, 8, 30, 66, 102-3, 105, 142,
  nick-names, 142,
  QAMH Millbank, 138, 141-3,
  sick parades, 118-9, 135

sportsmen, 30, 39, 51, 118, 135, 136
venereal diseases, 116
Royal Army Service Corps, 8-9, 30, 34, 94, 112,

S
Sherwood MM, Pte J.E, 63-4, 75
Sicily, 50, 64, 69, 70, 80,
　Operation Husky, 69, 81
Soviet Union, 18-9, 23, 33, 35, 145,
　Stalin, 34, 35,
　Eastern Front, 35, 64, 70, 114, 128, 129
Standen, Cissi, 16, 23-4, 26, 36, 38-39, 40, 97, 128, 139-40, 144,
Standen, Mary, 14-27, 34, 36-41, 44, 52, 53, 90-4, 96-7, 109-11, 119, 123, 128, 135, 137-47

T
Templer, Maj Gen Gerald, 97-106, 113
Trident Conference, 64, 69, 114
Tripartite Pact, 33, 39, 70

V
Volturno, 84, 86-8,
　crossing of, 87, 123

W
Wilder, Ivy, 15, 16, 23